The Perfect Life

The Perfect Life

 Lyric Essays

Peter Stitt

Tupelo Press T | P North Adams, Massachusetts

The Perfect Life: Lyric Essays.
Copyright 2013 Peter Stitt. All rights reserved.
First edition: October 2013.

Cover and text designed by Ann Aspell.
Cover art: Denis Versweyveld. Used courtesy of the artist
(http://denisversweyveld.com/).

Library of Congress Cataloging-in-Publication Data
Stitt, Peter.
 [Essays. Selections]
 The Perfect Life : essays / Peter Stitt. -- First edition.
   pages cm. -- (Tupelo Press's Life in Art Series)
 ISBN 978-1-936797-36-3 (pbk. original : alk. paper)
 I. Title.
 PS3569.T56A6 2013
 814'.54--dc23

                    2013025772

TUPELO PRESS
P.O. Box 1767
243 Union Street, Eclipse Mill, Loft 305
North Adams, Massachusetts 01247
Telephone: (413) 664–9611
editor@tupelopress.org / www.tupelopress.org

Tupelo Press is an award-winning independent literary press that publishes
fine fiction, nonfiction, and poetry in books that are a joy to hold as well as
read. Tupelo Press is a registered 501(c)3 nonprofit organization, and we
rely on public support to carry out our mission of publishing extraordinary
work that may be outside the realm of large commercial publishers. Finan-
cial donations are welcome and are tax deductible.

 Published with the support of the National Endowment for the Arts

The secret
Of this journey is to let the wind
Blow its dust all over your body,
To let it go on blowing, to step lightly, lightly
All the way through your ruins, and not to lose
Any sleep over the dead, who surely
Will bury their own, don't worry.

—James Wright, from "The Journey"

Contents

The Perfect Life

⟡ In Love Begins Responsibility

The most amusing moment of the evening came precisely at midnight, when Clara Johnson stood up and announced to her fellow students: "This has been great, but Mr. Wright and Professor Stitt have had a hard day and they need their sleep. It is time for us to say goodnight and go." *Oh, wow,* I thought to myself (this was in 1971), *what a classy gesture.* I had forgotten my request, made earlier that day, that the members of my class try to clear out by midnight so the visiting poet could get some sleep. James Wright's *Collected Poems* had just been published, and I had invited him to Middlebury College to give a reading.

Clara's gesture looked even more amusing by eight the next morning, after Jim had kept me up all night talking, drinking whiskey, reciting poems. I wish I could remember exactly what he said about Ray Livingston that night; his words were better, more paradoxical and surprising, than the version I will give. (Since his death Jim Wright has become James Wright, even to some of his closest friends; his widow, Annie, has never called him anything but James. But he was a Jim, and that is how I knew him.)

When Jim was denied tenure at the University of Minnesota, Ray Livingston found him a job in the English

Department at Macalester College, where Ray was chair. I never met Ray Livingston, but he sounds like a remarkable man: he was an outstanding teacher and scholar, a sensitive reader of literature, an admirer of the poetry of James Wright and a good friend to Jim. He seems to have had everything, and then he killed himself.

Looking back through the haze of alcohol, time, and cigarette smoke (Jim Wright was a heavy smoker), this is what I think I heard that night: "I loved Ray Livingston and I curse his soul. May he burn in hell for all eternity." I kept asking him to explain the contradiction, but he would only repeat his declaration and his curse.

We were friends before he became my teacher, and Jim did not commit suicide, at least not as the act is usually defined: he killed himself gradually, over fifty-two years, using alcohol and cigarettes. John Berryman was my teacher before he became a friend and he—after talking about it for most of his life—did finally and definitely kill himself, by jumping off a bridge at the age of fifty-seven. John's major work, *The Dream Songs,* is mostly about suicide; he talked about it in class also, and he talked about it in his home, in his hospital room, wherever one happened to see him. One of his truisms was this: the worst part of suicide is what it does to the survivors, the friends and loved ones, the ones the killer leaves behind, the ones who ask: *How could you do this to me?*

I DID NOT ASK THAT QUESTION ABOUT JOHN'S SUICIDE. I did not think I was important enough, for one thing—not to him (I cannot imagine that I showed up prominently on his radar, and certainly I was nowhere near his mind when he killed himself), not to the world; perhaps not even to myself. But he was important to me. When my friend Buddy Bell called from Minneapolis to give me the news, late in the afternoon of January 7, 1972, I was about to begin teaching an intensive month-long winter-term course in John Berryman's poetry; a couple of months earlier, I had finished editing my interview with him for the *Paris Review;* I was writing a book-length study of his work; I had published reviews and essays on his books of poems.

Over the next few months, I was distracted, nervous, depressed. I drank too much. At night I would take long, aimless walks, often ending up downtown, gazing from the bridge at the black water of the Middlebury River as it disappeared over the falls. I taught my classes and lived my life with a sense of desperation, as though I too were about to die; I lost weight, enough that friends began to ask about my health.

When summer came, I began writing this poem, later published in the *Georgia Review:*

WINTER SEARCH

> *Often he reckons, in the dawn, them up.*
> *Nobody is ever missing.*
> —DREAM SONG 29

The bell was tolling
When I awoke, and,

Seeing the thick snowflakes
Begin to fall again,

I called the men together.
Dressed in orange coveralls,

We spread out
In a comprehensive line.

The idea is always the same:
Keep the man on your right

Always in sight;
If you stumble over him,

Or if you find the slightest sign,
Stop and shout;

If you hear someone else shout,
Stop and shout.

We walked over the mountains
And through the valleys

In our usual silence;
No one stumbled,

No one stopped,
No one shouted.

When we returned at nightfall,
The man was still missing;

One man had somehow slipped away
In the snow-thickened dawn.

Although—in the Berryman poem from which I took my epigraph—John's protagonist, Henry, tries to convince himself that no one is missing, the truth is that at least one person was profoundly missing from John Berryman's world, and had been for many years. When John was twelve years old, his father apparently shot himself to death one morning just outside the (future) poet's bedroom window in Tampa, Florida. Most of the dream songs are concerned, directly or indirectly, with John Berryman's interpretation of that singular event and with Henry's reactions to it. The same could be said of John's life, and his death.

But not of my life. John Berryman was not my father, and I would not have chosen him to be. Nor was he my mentor. When I was halfway through my MA degree in English at the University of Minnesota, James Wright suggested that I apply for admission to the creative writing program at Syracuse. I asked John Berryman, then on leave for a year and teaching at Brown University in Rhode Island, to write a recommendation for me. He did not reply to several letters, but finally wrote something like this: "Dear Stitt, I am not a clearinghouse. Copy the enclosed and send it wherever you want. JB." His other note said (in about this many words) that I had been a brilliant student in his classes and had a bright future ahead of me. I sent a copy to Syracuse, but my application was denied—I am sure on its merits rather than because of John's off-handedness.

He was not a pleasant man: William Meredith once described him as the most self-conscious person he had ever known; I would say *self-absorbed*, utterly so. I suspect that his interest in me had only to do with my interest in—and promotion of—his work. His egotism made him seem cruel to those around him; his idea of office hours was to hold court for a group of adoring students, whose questions he would answer imperiously, while subtly mocking the questioners. I attended only one of those sessions, and I hated what he did.

Still, I felt a great loss when he died, and I miss him still today; it is easy to convince myself that I loved him, that I love him still. He was—is—a hero of mine and, in literary if not personal terms, he remains a model of many things I wish to be: he was the best teacher I ever had; he was a brilliant literary critic and student of literature (his brief review of two collections of short works by Henry James is based on his careful reading, and rereading, of all the novels, all the prefaces, all the criticism); he was a courageous, adventurous, experimental, learned, interesting, entertaining—albeit self-indulgent, prickly, self-promoting—poet.

THE SUICIDES I HATE THE MOST ARE THE ONES WHO kill someone else first, perhaps several someone elses, then themselves. Often the others they kill are innocent people—an abused wife or husband, a coworker, a group of complete strangers. While I do believe that a person has the right to take his or her own life, I do not believe any person has the right to take another person's life. But if that other person truly deserves to die, if the world, your world, will demonstrably be a better place without that person in it, then why should you not live on in this better, cleaner world, once you have gotten rid of that person? Even if you spent the rest of your life in prison, at least you would have the satisfaction that may go along with killing someone you deem truly bad.

So cases of this sort do not make sense to me. Similarly, if you are going to kill yourself anyway, I guess to escape from all those bad persons you also want to kill, why not kill just yourself and leave them to their fates? You will be without them in either case, and committing one murder has got to be easier than committing two, or several. There is also the possibility that, by killing your enemies along with yourself, you are actually taking them with you to the next world, and how would that help to solve your problems? The whole thing is idiotic, from a logical point of view, and I just hope that no one I know is thinking of killing me first, then taking his or her own life.

In most of your ordinary, everyday, garden-variety cases of suicide, I think a heavy battle must have been going on inside the person for a long time, perhaps a battle waged between the pain of real depression and a sense of responsibility, to oneself and to others. I suspect that a kind of selfishness, a selfishness born of self-pity, plays a crucial role. Certainly John Berryman was not thinking of his wife and daughters when he jumped off that bridge, though he may have been on the many other occasions when he stood at the brink and turned away. Perhaps he heard their voices in his head, asking from the future the question he had so often asked of his own father.

USING THE OBLIQUE AGENCY OF AN EXTENDED METAPHOR, "Winter Search" says that someone has disappeared from the speaker's life, from my life. It says that I have searched hard to find him—perhaps so I might save him—but that I have failed. It says that I have been abandoned, that I now feel entirely alone, and lonely; obviously the men that I call together to help me search are a figment of my imagination, a device made necessary by my choice of metaphor.

But that is not all. I think the poem says something else, something more important, at least to me: When the speaker says he sees "the thick snowflakes / Begin to fall again" just after he has heard the ominous tolling of that mysterious, otherworldly bell, I think he is saying that the terrifying cloud of depression that has enveloped him before is descending upon him once again. Thus the man he has failed to rescue by the end of the poem is not just John Berryman, but also himself. The poem is ultimately—and I guess obviously, given all that I have said—about my own depression.

When I lived in Middlebury, I always thought summer would be the best—the cleanest, least troublesome—time for suicide. I imagined that I would lie down on the dock by the old boathouse on the river (I imagined that there was a dock by the old boathouse on the river). I imagined that I would lie on my back with my head hanging over the water; that I would put the barrel of a shotgun in my mouth; that the mess would be carried away by the river; that my wife and children would not, at least, have to discover my body.

But what had they ever done to me to deserve such a thing? What had anyone? I cannot tell you for certain why someone would actually commit suicide; probably there are no logical, acceptable, reasons. In any case, I have not actually done it, so I do not know what my final reasons would be. But I can tell you why someone has chosen time after time *not* to commit suicide, however earnestly he may have wanted to. It is ultimately because of the echo of John Berryman's question ringing in my ears, the thought of others asking, *How could you do that to me?* I have never felt I had the right to hurt anyone so badly, and that is both the bad and the good news.

It is bad news because, in saying that, I am saying that I am not important enough to hurt you back, no matter how deeply I feel you have hurt me. It is good news because my statement implicitly recognizes that I do have some value, I do matter to those other people, who therefore must love me. And finally, I realize that I, as potential suicide, as potential survivor of my own suicide, ask John's question of myself, which is to say: *How could I do that to myself?* Hurtful others may or may not love me, but I have always felt that my ultimate duty to myself was to love myself; if no others can bring themselves to do this, at least I will do this for myself.

⌒ What Number Does He Wear?"

Nineteen-ninety-eight was a tough year for Tar Heel fans, fans of the University of North Carolina Tar Heel basketball team, of which I am proud to be one. We had a terrific team that year, with Antawn Jamison and Vince Carter anchoring a strong group of athletes. The team won the Atlantic Coast Conference title, but lost in the semi-final round of the NCAA tournament, the event that determines the national title. I was devastated by the loss, and as I groped in vain for solace, I wondered how one of my heroes, the great Billy Tubbs, would have handled this dilemma.

Among basketball fans, Billy Tubbs was famous for sounding, when he talked, exactly like Jack Nicholson. The coach of the Texas Christian University Horned Frogs in 1998, Tubbs had begun his career with the Cardinals of Lamar University and made his name with the Sooners of the University of Oklahoma. One night, after the Sooners had miraculously won a close game over a traditional rival, a reporter asked Tubbs, "Was God on your side tonight?"

Billy replied, "I don't know. What number does he wear?"

God's lack of interest in the University of Oklahoma basketball team dates back to 1862, when Congress finally passed the Homestead Act, authored by Rep. Galusha A. Grow. The act gave each settler the opportunity to purchase, at a nominal fee, a one-hundred-sixty acre section of the vast western lands owned by the United States government. Whenever a new tract was opened up, prospective homesteaders would gather at a starting line and race one another to grab the best parcels of land. Naturally there were cheaters, folks who would sneak onto the tract early, occupy the best sites, and claim them when the race began. Because these people got there too soon, they were called Sooners, and because much of this chicanery took place in Oklahoma, Oklahoma became known as the Sooner state. Had those early settlers been more honest, their teams would perhaps be known today as the Galushas.

And if Texas Christian University were a Catholic school, perhaps its athletic teams would be called the Friars (Providence), or the Crusaders (Valparaiso), or the Knights (Fairleigh Dickinson), the Red Storm (Saint John's), the Titans (University of Detroit), the Musketeers (Xavier), the Gael (Iona), the Hoyas (Georgetown), or the Billikens (Saint Louis).

Back when Georgetown was a hot team, everybody wanted to know, "What is a hoya?" Many Georgetown fans assume it is a fierce elfin creature of Irish extraction, but in reality a hoya is "an evergreen shrub of the milkweed family, a vine with star-shaped, waxy, white and pink flowers." Perhaps the name came to be applied to the Georgetown teams because of an ancient Jesuit belief, that the biblical burning bush may have been a hoya.

The name Billikens dates back only to the beginning of this century, when John Bender was coaching the Saint Louis University football team. Because of his roly-poly countenance and his squinty eyes, Bender was known as "Moonface" to his friends, one of whom, a barber named Charley McNamara, had a talent for drawing caricatures. McNamara's portrayal of Bender, posted on a local drugstore bulletin board, came out looking almost exactly like a billiken—the smiling "happy face" of the day. So popular was this figure that women wore billikens on their hatpins and men carried billiken watch fobs as good luck charms. Because of McNamara's drawing, the Saint Louis football team became known as Bender's Billikens. Local sportswriters took up the nickname with such enthusiasm that soon it was officially attached to all Saint Louis University athletic teams.

Texas Christian University may have taken its nickname from an epithet uttered by Pope Clement VII at the time of the Reformation. When Martin Luther emerged to join the so-called Gang of Johns (John Wycliff, John Huss, John Knox, John Calvin, and John Wesley), Clement contemptuously rechristened them "The Horned Frogs," perhaps because of the French blood rumored to be flowing in Luther's veins. Texas Christian University is in Fort Worth; down in Austin the people say, "If God is not a Longhorn, then why is the sunset Texas orange?" and in Chapel Hill they say, "If God is not a Tar Heel, then why is the sky Carolina blue?"

Why Why Wildcats? A Tar Heels Elegy

Tar Heels Midshipmen Fortyniners Flames
Running Rebels Tigers Spartans Eagles
Musketeers Huskies Gamecocks Spiders
Hoosiers Sooners Huskies Knights
Wildcats Colonels Volunteers Redbirds
Jaguars Illini Terrapins Aggies
Cornhuskers Razorbacks Runnin' Utes Dons
Mountaineers Owls Bearcats Lumberjacks
Jayhawks Panthers Racers Rams
Horned Frogs Seminoles Rebels Crusaders
Tigers Broncos Cardinal Cougars
Titans Red Storm Boilermakers Blue Hens
Blue Devils Highlanders Cowboys Colonials
Gaels Orangemen Bulldogs Lobos
Hurricanes Bruins Wolverines Wildcats
Minutemen Billikens Bulldogs *Wildcats*

Tar Heels Fortyniners Tigers Spartans
Huskies Spiders Hoosiers Huskies
Wildcats Redbirds Illini Terrapins
Razorbacks Runnin' Utes Mountaineers Bearcats
Jayhawks Rams Seminoles Crusaders
Broncos Cardinal Titans Boilermakers
Blue Devils Cowboys Orangemen Lobos
Bruins Wolverines Billikens *Wildcats*

Tar Heels Spartans Huskies Huskies
Wildcats Terrapins Runnin' Utes Mountaineers
Rams Crusaders Cardinal Boilermakers
Blue Devils Orangemen Bruins *Wildcats*

Tar Heels Huskies Runnin' Utes Wildcats
Rams Cardinal Blue Devils *Wildcats*

Tar Heels Runnin' Utes Cardinal *Wildcats*

Runnin' Utes *Wildcats*

Wildcats

If God Is Not a Rhode Island Ram, Then Why Are Sheep So Adorable?

After the Rams of the University of Rhode Island upset the Jayhawks of the University of Kansas in the second round of the tournament that year, Jim Harrick, coach of the Rams, explained: "There is a Heavenly Father and He was in the building this weekend, I'll tell you that, because it couldn't be more magical than it was."

A ram is a male sheep. A jayhawk is a sign of confusion. The mascot for the University of Kansas is a cartoon bird creature with a yellow, hawk-like beak and shifty eyes; it looks both aggressive and amused. But there is no jayhawk listed in any of the bird books I have consulted, and my encyclopedia explains that the word is derived from jayhawkers, which is what the free-state guerrilla

fighters, who were opposed to the proslavery "border ruf-
fians" during the struggle over Kansas in the years prior
to the Civil War, called themselves. Once the war itself
started, Jennison's Seventh Kansas Cavalry adopted the
nickname. Thus the proper mascot for the University of
Kansas Jayhawks might be a drawing of a scruffy back-
woods soldier with a six-day growth of whiskers on his
face.

March of 1998 must have been a busy month for the
Heavenly Father, with all those college basketball teams
clamoring for his support. Praying is endemic in sports,
even in the Atlantic Coast Conference, which most years
has the best basketball teams in the country. In *A March
to Madness*, his book on the ACC, John Feinstein points
out that Gary Williams of the University of Maryland
Terrapins "is the only coach in the ACC who does not
participate in some kind of pregame prayer with his play-
ers." This refusal may have cost Williams a game early in
1997. At the very time Williams was turning his back on
the Lord in the Terrapins locker room, this is what was
happening across the hall, in the Clemson Tigers locker
room: "...when Clemson's players and coaches knelt in
their pregame circle to say the Lord's Prayer, they were
so cramped that Barnes [Rick Barnes, head coach] almost
fell backwards into the shower room. The Tigers kneel
and pray both before and after every game." Perhaps it was
because of the humble posture of Rick "Shower Room"
Barnes that Clemson won that game, 67–63.

Not long after the Heavenly Father attended the Rhode
Island – Kansas game, with the results already noted, He

was called to Charlotte, where a man named Sean Gilbert was signing a contract to play for the Carolina Panthers of the National Football League. The contract was for $47.5 million over seven years. In 1997 Gilbert had turned down a similar deal with the Washington Redskins because God had told him it was not enough money.

And then, just one day after advising Gilbert to sign with the Panthers, the Heavenly Father was in Madison, Wisconsin, where another football player—the Reverend Reggie White of the Green Bay Packers—was addressing the Wisconsin state legislature. In his sermon on the greatness of the American people, Reggie White said that the plight of homosexuals should not be compared to that of blacks because homosexuality is "a decision, it's not a race. People from all different ethnic backgrounds also are liars and cheaters and malicious and back-stabbing." As for everyone else, they are OK in Reggie White's eyes, though each group has a different set of talents: black people are "gifted at worship and celebration"; white people are "good at organization"; Asians are able to "turn a television into a watch"; and Hispanics know how to "put twenty or thirty people in one home." This is what makes America such a great country. When Reverend Reggie was asked later why he had said all these things, he replied: "I have to say what God puts in my heart."

Perhaps it was because of all these commitments in the sporting world during March 1998 that the Heavenly Father missed out on what was happening to those little girls in Jonesboro, Arkansas, and to the Armenians in Kosovo, two notable massacres of the time.

WHEN I WAS A KID IN MINNEAPOLIS, I PLAYED BASKETBALL
on behalf of Mount Olivet Lutheran Church. Never once
did we pray over these games, and yet we won almost all
of them. Nor did Pastor Youngdahl ever lead a prayer on
our behalf in church on Sunday. But when I went with my
father and his pal Sammy Sampson to the games of the
Minneapolis Lakers, I would see George Mikan (graduate
of DePaul University, where he played for the Blue De-
mons) cross himself before every free throw. The Lakers
won most of their games in those days, and Mikan made
almost all his free throws: he shot them underhanded,
from between his legs. Sammy Sampson was Roman
Catholic and had been a minor league baseball catcher
when he was young. Now he coached an American Legion
baseball team and worked in the locker room at the Min-
neapolis Athletic Club, where the Lakers often practiced.
Once every week or two, George Mikan (or Jim Pollard or
Vern Mickelsen or Whitey Skoog or Pep Saul or one of the
other players) would give Sammy some free tickets, and
Sammy would take my dad and me to the game.

DURING THE SUMMER OF 1959, WHEN I WAS EIGHTEEN
years old and had just finished my freshman year at the
University of Minnesota, I had a summer job working as a
groundman on a line crew for the Northern States Power
Company. I was assigned to the Waconia division, about
thirty miles west of Minneapolis, and I drove out there
every day for work. I earned three dollars an hour, which
I remember because of the way my father exhorted me to
work hard: "Every minute that you work, the company

is putting five cents into your hand," he said. "Don't ever forget that."

I was required to become a member of the International Brotherhood of Electrical Workers and was happy to do so, for we had an excellent contract with the company. But Billy, the youngest of the three linemen on the crew, was certain that I would try to get out of paying my dues, so on the morning I received my first pay check, he made the driver, Norville Schmunke, stop the truck at the bank so I could cash my check. Then he took enough money from me to pay my dues and gave it to the union steward, who was our foreman. Perhaps I should have petitioned the Heavenly Father to save me from that unjust slur on my character.

Among other benefits, our contract provided that, when we were working outside of Waconia (as we did nearly every day), the company was required to buy our lunches. Every member of the crew but I lived in Waconia, and the idea was that they should be able to go home for lunch. If that was not practical, then the company would buy the noonday meal. We moved around quite a bit, but for the first few weeks of the summer, we worked ten or fifteen miles from Waconia and ate lunch at a small café in a nearby town.

One woman did all the cooking, serving, and cleaning up. She was pleasant, efficient, friendly, helpful, overworked, a thoroughly admirable person. And she was surrounded by her six children, ranging in age from a baby less than one year old to a boy about eight. If I had a few free minutes after eating, I would talk to the kids, play ball with them, whatever. I especially liked a funny, lively girl, who was six years old. The woman and her husband had only recently moved to this town, and he had taken a job at the feed mill. They were happy in this new community and working hard to make a good life for their children.

Schmunke, our driver, was a tank of a man, powerful and intelligent. I guess I respected him the most of everyone else on the crew, though he was a bit of a troublemaker. It was Schmunke who said to me, one hot afternoon after Billy and his pals had wrestled me to the ground, "Ira Shafer is the one who cut your bootlaces." Shafer was a big man, a lineman, and he seemed to dislike anyone who had too much fun. The person he really couldn't stand was Billy, but Billy would have won that fight. So Shafer, hanging from the top of a pole, would bounce insulators off my hard hat, knowing nothing would come of it.

I cannot remember everyone on that crew, but I do remember Chuck, the third of our three linemen, a thoughtful guy who rarely participated in the fooling around. He would tell me about weekend excursions with his wife and children, how he would pile everyone into the station wagon and head out for a lake or an amusement park. But not until after church on Sunday; Chuck never missed church. He liked me, perhaps because we were both outsiders, I the too-clever college kid who would leave in the fall, he the somber fellow who would never stop for a drink after work. I hope he came to be accepted after I left, for they were all good people, even Shafer. Billy, the youngest, would be in his seventies by now; some of them are surely dead. From my last day on the job to this day fifty-one years later, I have neither seen, nor heard of, nor heard from, any of them, nor will

I ever. But I miss them, and sometimes I think about the things we shared.

Like the blood of a morning when we happened upon a minor automobile accident. Schmunke stopped, and we hurried out of the truck, Billy in the lead, Shafer grabbing the first aid kit. It wasn't anything serious, but the people in the car that had gone off the road and hit a pole were happy to see us arrive, with our bandages and our concern.

Another person was not so lucky. It must have been in August. I arrived at work one morning and found the guys talking about someone who had died the night before. Gradually I caught on. The woman from that small-town café, the woman with the husband and six children, had driven to her church in a neighboring town for a meeting about a charitable project, collecting food for the poor or something like that, and on her way back home she was killed by a drunk driver whose car crossed the center line and hit hers head-on. The guys said the perpetrator was always drunk, always driving drunk, and he wasn't injured in the wreck.

I learned that the woman's husband fell into a terrible depression after his wife's death. Eventually he lost his job, and all he could do then was sit in a chair in the closed café and stare at the wall. He could summon no energy to care for the kids, who ran wild, fending for themselves. I wonder what happened to the bright little girl; she would be about fifty-seven by now.

And I wonder, have always wondered, about the Heavenly Father, where He was that night when the woman was driving home. Should He not have been watching over her, she who had spent her precious free time working on behalf of His children? Should He not have reached down and deflected that car before it could cross the center line? Should He not have gone to the bar where the drunk was drinking and put a stop to it somehow?

I mean—if He could look after the Rams in their epic battle with the Jayhawks; if He could secure for Sean Gilbert a better contract, over six million dollars per year; if He could write idiotic sermons for the Reverend Reggie White—if He could do all these things, then could He not have spared just one thought for that woman and her family, for that devastated father and those lonely kids?

Heavenly Father, I beseech you, if you exist, please go back in time and spare her, spare her and her husband and their children. Give them back their lives; allow them their happiness. If you must take someone, go back there and take me, that eighteen-year-old kid; take me and let her live. I beseech you, Heavenly Father, in the name of Sean Gilbert, in the name of Reggie White, in the name of Jim Harrick: take me and let her live.

A Philosophy of Composition

All I have to work with is a cloud—no, it is more like a huge, vaporous ball of chocolate-chip cookie dough, a cloudy ball of chocolate-chip cookie dough. Some people call them Toll House cookies, and I can go either way on that, though the name "chocolate-chip cookies" is more physically accurate and therefore easier for most people to understand—if they know what chocolate chips are, if they know what cookies are. "Toll House cookies" is another step removed from the reality of the actual cookies; I have not looked up the derivation of this name—I don't like to look things up; that is why I am stuck with my cookie dough—but I imagine that chocolate-chip cookies were customarily served, back then, in or at tollhouses—though why cookies would be distributed from tollhouses mystifies me. Certainly they are not so distributed today, at least not in my experience. Ultimately, however, it does not matter to me what these things are called—as Shakespeare once said, "What's in a name?," i.e., "That which we call a chocolate-chip cookie / By any other name would taste as sweet."

The reason I prefer "a huge, vaporous ball of chocolate-chip cookie dough" over a simple "cloud" for my metaphor is because I need those chocolate chips, and clouds do not contain chocolate chips. But "cloud" does imply uncertainty, a difficulty in perceiving—even the possibility that there is nothing out there to see—and I also need these elements of doubt. Not that I think that, in this particular case, there is *nothing* to see: I am certain that I attended John Burroughs Elementary School in Minneapolis from 1945 to 1951, am certain that I had seven different teachers there, and I am pretty sure of the names of five of those teachers and the grades they taught. Thus it was probably in Miss Fitzpatrick's (was that her name?) fourth-grade class that my friend Jim said to me, "You should be a cartographer when you grow up." He said this out of admiration for a map I had drawn of South America, which was both prettier and more accurate than his map of South America—though now that I think about that particular chocolate chip, I must confess that I am not certain it was South America—it could have been some other continent, or perhaps some individual country on a continent—but I do recall that we did an unusual amount with South America during my years at John Burroughs, so this seems a good-enough guess. In any case, a good writer uses specific details, and I am trying to be a good writer; thus saying "South America" even when I am not sure it was South America seems preferable to saying something like, "a map of some country or continent," even though that may be more accurate.

I am also not sure of exactly when I decided that I wanted to be a writer and not a cartographer—nor an engineer, a tap dancer, a physicist, a cable car operator, or a counterman in a donut shop—but that is indeed what I decided to do, perhaps as early as when I was in the fifth grade and writing stories about Ezra Hondo, Detective. But I did not announce my decision until twelfth grade, shortly before I matriculated at the University of Minnesota as an electrical engineering major. When, or even if, I actually became a writer is also an uncertain matter, but that is not what concerns me now. What I wish to debate with myself on this occasion are purely factual matters, things to do mostly with *why*, but also with *what* and *how*. One thing I know is that my writing in general is based, however loosely, on facts. Sometimes on facts that can and should be looked up, but more often on the kinds of facts that show up as chocolate chips in the doughy glop of my memory. You could call this kind of writing *creative nonfiction*, or you could call it *literary nonfiction*, or you could call it *pathologically delusional bull hockey*. But no matter what you call it, it is most definitely the wrong kind of writing to be doing at this particular time in these particular United States of America, and the reason for that has to do with the use, or the misuse, of facts.

"Fact is the underpinning of morality."

— Suzannah Lessard

A few years back a writer named H. G. Bissinger made a lot of noise up in New York City over what he considered the blatant lies contained in—indeed, built into by the author of—John Berendt's best-selling nonfiction book,

Midnight in the Garden of Good and Evil. I don't know why it took Mr. Bissinger so long to get around to this subject (the book was published five or six years before Mr. Bissinger wrote his critique), but he obviously came to feel strongly enough about it to have formed a faction of nonfiction writers dedicated to the proposition that all facts reported in a work of nonfiction should be verifiably true. I read *Midnight in the Garden of Good and Evil* several years ago myself, and I loved it; the movie, though entertaining, was not nearly as good. In his afterword, Mr. Berendt confesses that he changed some of the facts while writing his account of a murder and a trial that occurred in Savannah, Georgia. Specifically, he says he changed the names of some of the people, altered somewhat the chronology of events, and invented at least one conversation. He also put quotation marks around the words spoken by the participants in that phony conversation—which is an issue to the truth faction because Frank McCourt did not use quotation marks when he recreated or fabricated conversations in his own best-selling nonfiction book, *Angela's Ashes. Angela's Ashes* is an even more terrific book than *Midnight in the Garden of Good and Evil,* but it has not been made into a movie.

Of his own nonfiction book, *A Prayer for the City,* Mr. Bissinger says all the facts are absolutely true. He went through hell writing this book, and it is not even a best seller: "Writing books is hard," he says. "And if you're trying to get it right, you really do suffer with the facts you have. Believe me, I went through a lot of days of depression and self-doubt, but one thing I was not going to do is make it up." I am very much in sympathy with what Mr.

Bissinger says here; my own mother taught me only two things, but she taught them well: "Never tell a lie," she said, "and don't ever punch out a woman." I never saw my mother punch out a woman, but she did punch me out plenty of times, and this is an absolutely true fact. As for lying, knowing what I know now about people who lay down rigid rules for others to follow, I would not be surprised to learn that my mother lied through her teeth on many occasions.

In a moment of intense, almost *fictional,* creativity, Mr. Bissinger created a new definition for the word *faction,* which he applied as an insulting label to nonfiction books that contain fictional, or untrue, facts. Unfortunately, his coinage of this word seems to show him capitulating to the enemy in his battle, for faction so used is an ersatz, or nonfactual, word. In any case, the faction of writers that Mr. Bissinger has formed is a fervent group indeed, as is evident in a comment made by my friend Suzannah Lessard as she was announcing the winner of the prize in nonfiction at the National Book Awards dinner in 1997, long before I met her: "Fact is the underpinning of morality." Now it occurs to me that both Ann Landers and her lesser-known sister Abigail Van Buren—when they were alive, and unless I am badly misreading the texts—disagree with this lofty standard. It would be hard to find a pair of people more devoted to morality and to the truth and to all conjunctions between them than Ann and Abby, and yet during their careers advising the lovelorn, they regularly condoned the use of the white lie in matters of adultery, at least when the adulterer has repented and rejoined her spouse. Nothing will be gained by telling the truth in these situations, Ann and Abby say; let sleeping dogs lie. I know in my heart that, on an ideal or abstract level, I agree with Suzannah Lessard (whose comment echoes one made earlier by Ezra Pound), at the same time as, on a more practical level, I agree with Ann and Abby. Mostly, however, I sympathize with the practice of John Berendt, whose handling of facts is so much closer to my own.

A Picture Is Worth a Thousand Words

In essence, what a cartographer does is draw pictures of the land, pictures that increase in strict moral value in direct proportion to their accuracy; what a good mapmaker wishes to record is the literal truth, the exact facts. I think this is also the primary impulse behind much of what is called *outsider art,* the kind of art, for example, practiced by the Dutch creator of free-hand drawings, Anthonius Hendrikx—whose work was once featured and briefly discussed in an issue of the distinguished literary journal, the *Gettysburg Review,* of which I am the editor. Mr. Hendrikx said that he did his drawings so that later generations would know what life on the farm was like in his day. Drawings, he felt, would be more accurate than any string of words he could hope to put together. And yet many of his drawings are also full of words, as is so often the case with outsider art, art by artists with only a "primitive" understanding of their art. Toon (as his friends called him) Hendrikx's goal was accuracy; he wanted to get it right; he wanted to tell the truth about the facts, the details, the objects and implements and events of life as he lived it for sixty-six years on the farm—*his* farm, the farm at the Donk, that farm and that farm only.

I am strongly attracted to outsider art, for its inno-
cence, its naiveté, its childlike belief in the truth of out-
ward reality—and for its courage, the willingness of the
artist to announce to a skeptical world, "This is how it is or
was." I also happen to love—well, *admire* would be a more
accurate word—the epitome of accurate, factual, truthful
drawing, the kind you find sometimes in automotive or
engineering magazines, mechanical drawings that repro-
duce the proportions, details, and design of the insides
of machines with meticulous precision. Nothing could
be truer, more revealing, than these drawings, not even
a photograph of the outside of a car, for that would show
only the surface, while the machine drawing strips away
all the surfaces to show what is really in there. And yet
there is something profoundly false, untrue, and fictional
about all pictorial representations, as Rene Magritte dem-
onstrated conclusively when he wrote, outsider-like, at
the bottom of his faithful-to-life painting of a pipe, *"Ceci
n'est pas une pipe"*—this is not a pipe. And it is not a pipe,
no matter that it looks exactly like one.

And even if it were a pipe, one still may still wonder,
What is a pipe?

> "The famous pipe. How people reproached me
> for it! And yet, could you stuff my pipe?"

> — Rene Magritte

"**pipe** (pip) n. [ME. < OE. < Wgmc. **pipa* < VL. *Pipa* <
L. *pipare*, to cheep, chirp, peep, of echoic orig.] 1. a cylin-
drical tube, as of reed, straw, wood, or metal, into which
air is blown as by the mouth for making musical sounds

by the vibration of an air column . . . 2. any of the tubes in an organ that produce the tones 3. a boatswain's whistle used to signal the ship's crew 4. a high, shrill sound, as of a voice, birdcall, etc. 5. [*often pl.*] the vocal organs, esp. as used in singing 6. a long tube of clay, concrete, metal, wood, etc., for conveying water, gas, oil, etc., or for use in construction 7. a tubular organ or canal of the body; esp., [*pl.*] the respiratory organs 8. *a)* a somewhat cylindrical deposit of ore *b)* an opening into a volcano's crater 9. anything tubular in form 10. *a)* a tube with a small bowl at one end, in which tobacco, etc., is smoked *b)* enough tobacco, etc., to fill such a bowl 11. *a)* a large cask for wine, oil, etc., having a capacity of about two hogsheads, or 126 gallons *b)* this volume as a unit of measure *c)* such a cask with its contents *12. [Slang] something regarded as easy to accomplish."

> "Words, book-words, what are you?"
>
> — Walt Whitman

Not long ago I wrote an essay about basketball and God, specifically the curious fact that God often seems to favor —or is said to favor, or felt to favor—one college basketball team or coach over another. If you are reading the essays in this book sequentially, then you are already familiar with that essay. One person who read that essay at the time of its publication in a distinguished literary journal wrote a letter addressed "to the Editor, the *Gettysburg Review*," which I found curious since he obviously had a copy of the issue in his hand, and since the editor's name is printed rather prominently in every issue of the magazine, and since my correspondent presented himself as being devoted to factual truth, to looking things up and getting them right. I am not going to reveal this man's name (I haven't asked him for permission to quote from his letter), but the organization listed on his letterhead— International Security Studies at Yale University—makes him sound like someone to be listened to when the subject of discussion is the accuracy of one's facts.

As for factual mistakes, my correspondent says I made four of them: First, I was wrong in identifying Valparaiso (the Crusaders) and Fairleigh Dickinson (the Knights) as Catholic universities; as Mr. International Security Studies correctly says in his letter, "Valpariso is . . . Lutheran," and Fairleigh Dickinson is nondenominational. Having won this skirmish, however, he goes on to assert that "Forty Niners and Flames are not college nicknames," and he is wrong on both counts here: the nickname for the teams at the University of North Carolina at Charlotte is indeed 49ers (as it also is for those at Long Beach State), and the nickname at the University of Illinois at Chicago is indeed the Flames (just as at Liberty University).

The other two "facts" over which my correspondent and I disagree are more complex. In response to my creatively humorous speculation about the nickname of the Georgetown Hoyas—"a hoya is 'an evergreen shrub of the milkweed family, a vine with star-shaped, waxy, white and pink flowers.' Perhaps the name came to be applied to the Georgetown teams because of an ancient Jesuit belief, that the biblical burning bush was a hoya"—my correspondent explained correctly that "The dictionary definition of a 'Hoya' is as you say, but at Georgetown they claim it is Latin slang for a rock." And in response to my explanation for the nickname "the Horned Frogs": "Texas Christian University may have taken its nickname from an epithet uttered by Pope Clement VII at the time of the Reformation. When Martin Luther emerged to join the so-called Gang of Johns (John Wycliff, John Huss, John Knox, John Calvin, and John Wesley), Clement contemptuously rechristened them 'The Horned Frogs,' perhaps because of the French blood thought to be flowing in Luther's veins"—my correspondent reports that "Knox, Calvin, Wesley all 'emerged' after Luther."

Again my correspondent is correct on both counts, though he did overlook my attempts to create humor, puerile though it may have been, through a series of blatant falsifications. With regard to the Hoyas, I tried to indicate my intentions by using the word "perhaps." With regard to the Horned Frogs, I am surprised that Mr. International Security Studies did not question my other "facts"—the supposed French blood of Luther, the bogus appellation "Gang of Johns," and the statement attributed to Pope Clement VII—all of which blatantly and intentionally work to undermine the underpinnings of morality. Such is the nature of creative nonfiction, at least the variety of it practiced by me.

"This is not my beautiful house."

— David Byrne

I think it really began when I gave that speech nominating Kingsley Johnson to be president of the Student Council, or something. Here is the story: At my high school, Washburn High in Minneapolis, we had a teacher everyone assumed was gay, and even if he was not gay, he was a real priss, always insisting that we answer his questions with exact facts based on the actual text, which in his case was written by Shakespeare. I remember my one shining moment in his class. For some reason, he was trying to get Mr. Casey to tell him the sound of the letter *d*, and Mr. Casey did not know what to say. After a lot of badgering of Mr. Casey, Mr. Blackmur, for that was his name, turned to the dumbest kid in class—me—and asked him the question. I was busy creating fictions about cheerleaders, or dreaming about trees in springtime, or something, but—while trying to gather my wits—I stalled by saying "Duh." Mr. Blackmur was ecstatic: "That's it. Now why cannot you figure these things out, Mr. Casey?"

Anyway, when it came time to give my speech, I decided to become a humorist. So I began by saying, slowly and in my most formal tones, "Students . . . Faculty . . . Administrators . . . Office   Employees . . . Janitors . . . Food Service Workers . . . And Mr. Blackmur . . ." and was interrupted by crescendos of knowing laughter. Later that day, some of Mr. Blackmur's acolytes—he was the type of teacher who had acolytes—nabbed me in the hall and said that Mr. Blackmur wanted to see me. I was terrified, but all he wanted to say was, "Congratulations. Who ever would have thought you would come up with something good? What do you want to be when you grow up?" "A writer," I instinctively replied, much to my own surprise. "Well, if you can use that sense of timing in your writing," Mr. Blackmur replied, "then you will be a good writer." So I went off to college to study electrical engineering and eventually became one of America's leading literary critics.

Which is why—when one of my own students asked, "What should I be when I grow up, I like to write?," and I asked her back, "What sort of thing do you like to write?," and she answered me back, "I love to write about literature"—I said, "Oh God, for the love of Mary, Joseph, and Baby Jesus, don't do that!" What I meant was this: "If you wish to be a writer, then you must want to communicate with other human beings roughly as intelligent as you are. But nobody reads literary criticism, though it is still an honorable thing to write. So write something else instead—memoirs, fiction, faction, poetry, whatever. Just don't waste your life writing literary criticism."

In September of 1997 I published my second book of literary criticism, *Uncertainty and Plenitude: Five Contemporary Poets*. It took me ten years to write this book, and the only time I could find to work on it was between 4:00 and 8:00 every weekday morning. I wanted it to be a beautiful book, so I paid to have a painting by John Winship reproduced on the dust jacket. After waiting a full year to receive the acclamation that I think I so richly deserve, I received in the mail a copy of my first and only review. It is a good review, and I am delighted to have it, but I am not entirely sure that the reviewer read the book as carefully as I would have liked. Here is what I consider to be her faction, her fiction based upon the fact of my text:

In his introduction, supporting his thoughts with evidence from post-Newtonian physics, Stitt outlines the reasons he sees uncertainty and plenitude as being uniting themes of these writers. Throughout the book he works to unite the poets' work to these themes. But if there is a weak element of the book, it is this insistence to bring the writing back to the themes and to compare one writer to another. Each poet has established an individual voice and created a unique body of work that stands on its own, so the imposed framework seems constricting rather than liberating.

The point of my thesis was precisely to undermine the certainty of an ordinary thesis; my title means to say that *everything*—poetry, prose, facts, fictions—is uncertain, and there sure is a lot of entertaining *everything* in contemporary poetry. Let me quote the final sentences of my chapter on John Ashbery:

> I am convinced—certain—of the truth of everything that I say in this essay; but what I am most fundamentally saying is that truth is uncertain, in studying poetry as in studying the quantum world. Thus I am conscious of being a participant, a creator, of the world that I perceive. I hope therefore, that no one will be surprised that my own method is based solidly—oh, very solidly indeed!—on the principle of uncertainty.

In other words, there are no reliable themes in the work of these poets, certainly no theme of uncertainty to bring it and them back to, time after time. I was writing *faction*, except that I was not making up the facts. I was instead insisting that everything everyone thinks is a fact is in fact a fiction, that this is the nature of our being. The irony, to my eyes, is both rich and amusing, and it just goes to show you the truth of everything that I have said right here.

Love, Sex, Insurance, Literature

He Took the Road Less Traveled By

Here is a story that happens to be true: A guy I know fell in love with a woman, a vice president of a major American insurance company, when he saw her leaning over the counter of a bookstore working something out about her credit card one night in 1985, and this was at a poetry reading in Houston, to which she had miraculously—his word—come searching for something that would resurrect her soul from the withering death it was suffering day by day in the corporate world, and he turned out to be it—so she told him later—rather than the poetry. The poetry, she said, was good, but not that good.

Eventually they started talking about marriage, and he was one of those guys who taught literature at a university and thought he was really a writer except that he never had time to write, poor thing, and out of the depths of her burgeoning love, she suggested that maybe he should quit his job and stay home and write, and she would keep climbing up the fire pole of success at the insurance company while making more than enough money to support all of them—for there was a youngster involved, I think he

38

was in fifth grade at the time—but the guy was a gentle-
man of the old school, and he said no; he would get a
different job in a different state, and she could quit her
job for the good of her soul, and they would live happily
ever after, so they did that, and he still doesn't have time
to write, but her soul began thriving, and the youngster
eventually graduated from a fine college and has gone on
to several careers.

Back near the beginning of this now-defunct relation-
ship, the woman told the guy a story that he thought he
might be able to use during his career as a writer: It seems
the company she worked for had a CEO who considered
himself to be a path-breaking corporate philosopher, the
kind of CEO who would think it appropriate to write up—
well, actually speak into a Dictaphone—a management
system designed to guide the behavior of all his employees
and enhance the profitability of the company, so he did
this, and the company and its employees thrived: None
of them ever again majored in minors; none of them wal-
lowed about in the slough of mere facts lying at the bot-
tom of the ladder when they should have been oinking
theory from the top; none of them let their little brains
crawl into a pigeonhole and never fly back out. Best of all,
however, every one of these employees ever after took the
road less traveled by, and that has made all the difference.

They all of them did that, tromped on down that one
less-traveled road, because of this: On the portentous and
futurific day when the CEO presented his management
system to an assemblage of all the employees of his com-
pany, he also delivered an inspiring speech illustrating
how the principles embodied in that system, along with

a certain frame of mind—*the Robert Frost frame of mind*—
had made him the man he was, standing before them now,
rapturing their attention, a man rich, powerful, forceful,
commanding, masterful, triumphant, victorious, van-
quishing, creative, inventive, brawny, vehement, virile,
jaunty, impetuous, wise, profound, philosophical, re-
fined, urbane, debonair, theoretical, cultivated, cultured,
buoyant, elegant, poignant, cogent, trenchant, eloquent,
suave, resourceful, well-groomed, omnipotent, erudite,
unbowed—and independent, above all independent, a
lone rider of the purple spreadsheet, a pioneer, a bush-
whacker, a trailblazer, a lone scout way out ahead of the
crowd, traipsing where no others would traipse, a Robert
Frost kind of a guy, venturing into the great dismal swamp
with neither geographical terrain map nor a local redneck
to guide him, for he was out there on his own, he was
taking the road less traveled by, he was making all the
difference.

When the woman who had leaned over the store
counter working something out about her credit card
finished telling this story to the literature professor guy
who thought he could be a writer, he fell so deeply in love
that he vowed to propose marriage to her the very next
time he saw her step off the bus from Houston to Austin,
which would also be the first and last time he would ever
see her do that, for he found in her story the connection
he had been pursuing for much of his working life, the
umbilical cord that he always knew must exist between
poetry, his personal passion, and the rest of the world, in-
cluding the insurance industry, which was her ill-chosen
passion, the connection that would allow him to bring

poetry to the people, to become rich and famous for doing so, to take his place on the couches of the already and burgeoning rich and famous, beside Dave and Jay and Conan and Craig and perhaps even that other Frost, David, the British one, or of Tom Snyder, the ironist's ultimate dream, and thanks to her, thanks to that skinny, beautiful, white-haired young woman with the high forehead and the stray fifth-grader, the woman who had lost the keys to her Honda and was chronically unable to balance her checkbook, he now knew that Robert Frost was the cord or string or wire, the duct or strapping tape who made that connection possible, thanks to his great poem, "The Road Not Taken."

Is Money a Kind of Poetry?

Unless that duct-tape connection were to be found in the life of Wallace Stevens...

This is the thought that jostled him awake that very night from dreams of wedded bliss—for Wallace Stevens, another great American poet of the twentieth century, had also been a vice president of a major American insurance company, namely the Hartford Group, and maybe he was the key to the road so seldom traveled (it is essential to be accurate in matters of this sort, for scholars will likely get involved, and everyone knows what they are like if someone gets a fact wrong, even if the imaginative construct of which this fact is merely an insignificant part is brilliant, a stroll down a road not just less traveled by but one never before traveled by at all, an entirely original road-n-stroll; in such cases scholars will turn vicious indeed), so the guy looked into it the first chance he had, which came nearly fifteen years later, when he, now at long last himself blossoming as a writer, began again to think about this very topic, in preparation for writing about it, and what he found is that Wallace Stevens, far from building a road or routing a freeway from poetry to the real world, did everything he could to make the sundering between them even more acutely pronounced, for Stevens seemed pretty much convinced that, were his employers to learn of his avocation, they would probably fire him for an excess of creative imagination, and the guy found himself agreeing with Stevens if on no firmer basis than what Joan Richardson points out in the preface to her two-volume biography, that although Stevens was "considered the dean of surety claims in the country," he also was "afraid . . . that he might lose his job as vice president of the insurance company where he had been employed for almost forty years were he not to be at his desk every day."

So no, Stevens was not fooled by any of this idealistic dreaming of rapprochement between poets and insurance executives, and by extension to the world of everyday people, no more than was the guy now, for he had suddenly remembered (smacking his forehead with the palm of his left hand) the lesson taught him by his dear friend and mentor—I'll call him Howard—then chair of the Department of American Literature at Middlebury College, who set him straight one evening back in 1969 or '70 when the guy made a casual remark revealing that he, like the CEO, was understanding Frost's poem only on its surface level, the level where no irony is operating,

the level on which Frost claims proudly to have taken
the road less traveled by, whereas Howard actually knew
Frost, whose cabin in Ripton, Vermont, was mere miles
from Howard's home in Middlebury and mere hundreds
of yards from Bread Loaf, where Frost had founded and
Howard had attended and then hung out at for many
years, the Bread Loaf School of English (of which the
guy was himself somewhat after the time of this current
anecdote the acting director *pro tempore*) and therefore
Howard knew much more about the poem than the guy
did, and so Howard explained to him that the speaker of
the poem was not Robert Frost but a self-regardful man
who would one day be a pompous old fool, the kind of
fool who would brag about doing things his way despite
the opposition of most of the civilized world, all of whom
counseled then and evermore taking the road most trav-
eled by, the one everyone else took, and that the guy
could figure this out for himself, Howard said, by read-
ing the poem with greater care, in which case he would
surely notice that Frost himself has his speaker himself
actually admit that no difference could be ascertained
between the two roads, "for that the passing there / Had
worn them really about the same // And both that morn-
ing equally lay / In leaves no step had trodden black,"
which is to say that the pompous fool was more or less
making all this up just to make himself look, in the eyes
of his listeners, like a pioneer, a bushwhacker, a trailblaz-
er, all of that. The guy was mortified hearing this, for he
knew even then that he would never be tenured at that
estimable college, but at least he had picked up another
anecdote that would prove valuable if and when he ever

did get some time to write about all of this, which apparently is about now.

The Tyranny of Tidy Minds

The truth is that they hate poetry; they think poets are fags, queers, limp-wristers, persons of doubtful masculinity, be the poets actually male, in which case the doubt is that they have enough of this masculinity stuff, or female, in which case the doubt is that they have too much of it, and Stevens was right to keep his secret, and the CEO who proudly quoted Frost's poem was an idiot, a moron, a fool, and a player of golf caught in the process of proving, by his very use of the poem, that he belonged securely among the *most conventional* of his ilk, the ones like him who all dressed in designer suits, had their hair coiffed and sprayed daily, and wore—still wear, I swear, the guy and his ex-wife swear—clear polish on all their fingernails, so now which kettle is it exactly that is calling the pot black, and who is it who is marching in lockstep down the most worn road of all?

It really is just a question of conventionality, a question of basing your moral and aesthetic and even athletic judgments not on originality and creativity and just plain old quality but on adherence to the majority standard, which is why so many otherwise sensible people used to hate John McEnroe, the tennis player, and Dennis Rodman, the basketball player, even though they are two of the best ever to play their respective sports, because they occasionally would or will behave in nonconventional ways, impolite ways, ways that some people's mothers would never have let them behave, and often these passers of judgment are the most boring people of all, the least creative, the ones most trapped in little boxes or wallowing in the muck, and it is not a good thing when some of these truly little people have power over some of the truly big ones, the creators, the ones who really and truly did see a different path and chose to wander down it; for example, Edward Connery Lathem's metaphorically criminal ascendancy over the great American poet Robert Frost.

Donald Hall told this story in *The Atlantic Monthly* back in March of 1982, how Edward Connery Lathem, who was the head librarian at Dartmouth College, in editing for publication *The Poetry of Robert Frost*, had made "1,117 changes for which he offer[ed] no textual sources, an average of 3.4 for each poem," despite the plain facts that: 1) in Hall's words, "an editor's task is to represent the author's intent insofar as the editor can establish it"; 2) Frost himself was well versed in all matters pertaining to the English language, including grammar, punctuation, and usage; and 3) therefore, "If [the poet] had wished to sprinkle his lines with new commas, as one might salt a roast, he could have penciled them into his reading copy. If he had wished to add a question mark, or to delete a hyphen, it would have been simple to do so. In the absence of alterations, his repeatedly printed texts suggest intention," all of which seems plain enough, except that Frost's creative and intentional "inconsistencies in punctuation and his deviations from standard practice bother a tidy mind. So a tidy mind will find relief in Lathem's revision, which insists on consistency to the exclusion of other criteria."

The Poetry of Robert Frost was first published in 1969, six years after the death of the poet, and was the only volume of Frost's collected poems still available in 1982, though since then the Library of America has issued its own standard volume restoring the poems to the form in which Frost wanted them printed, and that is great news for Frost and his admirers, but the reputation of Edgar Allan Poe has still never recovered from the lies told about him by the tidy-minded Rufus Wilmot Griswold, and although Jane Austen and Emily Dickinson have had at least a sort of textual rehabilitation, sex and politeness remain problems in both cases.

Cutting Off Jane Austen's Head

Returning to the guy, whose history I seem to be presenting in reverse chronological order this time around, he spent much of the summer of 1962, or maybe '63, lying on a beach beside Cedar Lake in Minneapolis reading and rereading and then rereading again the Modern Library edition of *The Novels of Jane Austen*, and for many years he wondered how the perfect little Virgin-Mary-of-a-Pippi-Longstocking Jane Austen described in biographies could have written those deliciously, bitingly ironic books, and his question was answered just this last spring when he read the recent biography by David Nokes, who makes two shocking points pertinent to this matter, the first of which is that Jane's beloved sister Cassandra burned most of Jane's letters shortly after Jane's death, with the express purpose of getting rid of anything in the least bit sarcastic or romantic, and the second of which is that

Cassandra and a whole host of other Austens created and then perpetuated what I would like to call the "God's-in-His-Heaven-all's-right-with-the-world" version of Jane's life and character.

Happily, Cassandra did not burn any other of Jane's unpublished writings—even though Jane and Cassandra's niece Caroline Austen (in the words of David Nokes) "disapproved of the notion that any of Jane's early satirical writing should be published; 'one knows not how it might be taken by the public,' she wrote"—some of which were finally issued under the title *Love and Freindship [sic] and Other Early Works* (with a preface by G. K. Chesterton) by Chatto & Windus in 1923 (a copy of which a valued "freind" of the guy's recently presented to him, thus inspiring both his revisiting of the works of Jane and the present scribbling)—though other relatives did immediately begin the process of cleansing Jane's reputation, for example her brother Henry, who said of Jane that, "faultless herself, as nearly as human nature can be, she always sought in the faults of others, something to excuse, to forgive or forget"—this even though Jane herself had once proudly announced that she had "endeavoured to give something like the truth with as little incivility as I could"; quite a different aim.

My own favorite sterilizing characterization of Jane was penned by her nephew, James Edward Austen, in whose glazed eyes "she was a humble, believing Christian. Her life had been passed in the performance of home duties, and the cultivation of domestic affections, without any self-seeking or craving after applause. Her needlework...was excellent, and might almost have put a sewing-machine to shame"—an observation, this last, that was echoed by James Edward's sister Caroline, who pointed out that Jane was "a great adept at overcast and satin stitch"—though I must confess that I grow crossest of all when I compare this statement by Richard Arthur Austen-Leigh—"I have no reason to think that she ever felt any attachment by which the happiness of her life was at all affected"—with David Nokes's accounts of Jane's two intense but tragically brief relationships with men whom she probably loved (though the letters that would prove this went up in smoke, thanks to Cassandra), namely Tom Lefroy—from whom Jane was expecting a proposal of marriage when "his family, taking sudden fright at the prospect of an engagement between this young and penniless couple, had stepped in to prohibit any further contact between them," with the result that they never again set eyes upon one another—and the unnamed but apparently prosperous enough gentleman of whom Caroline reported, "the impression left on Aunt Cassandra was that he had fallen in love with her sister," and of whose sudden and mysterious demise Louisa Austen said, "He and Jane fell in love with each other, but instead of his arriving [for a promised visit with the sisters], they received a letter announcing his death"—though the most recent development on the question of Jane's affectional relations, that she had an intimate homosexual relationship with Cassandra (in clear anticipation of which, perhaps, their mother had said, when the two girls were but tykes, "If Cassandra were to have her head cut off, Jane would insist on having hers cut off too"), makes me quite extraordinarily cross as well.

The Incubus of Good Intentions

And yet, hard as the creative path may have been, post-humously and/or humously, for Robert Frost and Wallace Stevens and Jane Austen, it has been still worse for Emily Dickinson—though before I get into that I think I should catch up with myself by telling you what the guy I have been talking about knows about the sex lives of Stevens and Frost, which in the case of Stevens is more than he wants to know, for although one might think Stevens would have been pretty active sexually, given not just that he wrote poetry, but also because of his martini-swilling–at-the-Canoe-Club, off-to-Florida-with-the-boys lifestyle and the fact that his wife Elsie was beautiful enough to have sat as the model for the figure of Liberty on the Liberty dime, he suffered from a chemical imbalance that drastically reduced his sex drive; but Frost's is a different story, as biographer after biographer seems determined to prove in ever-greater detail, though all the guy knows firsthand is the gossip he heard up at Bread Loaf and then read in the monumental biography by Lawrence Thompson: that in his late years Frost was regularly screwing his secretary at the cabin in Ripton, despite his warm friendship with her husband, to whose bosom she repaired each evening after being romped upon by Robert.

To Emily's sex life I shall return, for the guy thinks he knows a lot about that too, but first there is the matter of the editing of her poems, which makes a far more grievous story than the one about Frost and Lathem, for this started earlier and went on much longer and involved actual and unauthorized rewriting of a noxiously conventionalizing sort, for the fact is that only seven of Emily's poems were published during her lifetime, and all of those were changed by their editors, including even the one (now known as number 214) printed by Samuel Bowles, one of Emily's ostensible lovers, in the *Springfield Daily Republican*, who rewrote the last two lines of the first stanza—

> I taste a liquor never brewed—
> From Tankards scooped in Pearl—
> Not all the Frankfort Berries
> Yield such an Alcohol!—

to read "Not Frankfort berries yield the sense / Such a delicious whirl"—probably in order to make the rhyme exact rather than slant, even though Emily was truly a bushwhacking pioneer in the field of slant rhyme—which she practically invented, thereby adding great subtlety to the possible uses of sound in poetry.

Bowles's change, like many of the others made to Emily's poems, also works in the direction of simplifying, clarifying, demystifying—*literalizing*—her metaphors, which is a disgusting and pitiful thing for an editor to do, given the condescension it implies toward his readers and the contempt it shows he has for the poet, apparently for being smarter than he, which, I am delighted to say, did not bother George Whicher about Emily Dickinson, who found "the gnomic concision of [her] poems [to be] a continual stimulus to mental alertness. She does not encourage a dreamy half-attention on the reader's part"—and this is the same George Whicher who also answered some of the stupid things that have been said about Emily's use of slant rhyme by observing, "It is safe to conclude . . . that she knew exactly what she was doing and did it with full intent," thank you very much.

Like Jane Austen, Emily Dickinson had a sister, Lavinia, who burned her letters, in this case all of the ones at her disposal rather than some—and this at Emily's own specific request—though Lavinia could not bring herself to burn—as Emily had also asked her to—the more than nine hundred poems she found in Emily's desk, neatly if almost illegibly handwritten and gathered into small bundles of about fifteen poems each—so instead she carried them next door to Susan Gilbert Dickinson, wife of Edward Dickinson, Emily and Lavinia's brother, with the thought that perhaps Sue—another of Emily's ostensible lovers—would want to prepare them for publication, but Sue, who possessed a good bit of repressed anger directed at her sisters-in-law for a reason known to the guy—could not make up her mind what to do and, after some months had gone by, Lavinia retrieved the manuscripts and delivered them instead to Mabel Loomis Todd—a literary woman married to the professor of biology at Amherst College (of which Edward Dickinson was treasurer, as had been his father before him)—who readily agreed to undertake the task and immediately enlisted the aid of the powerful Bostonian literary lion Thomas Wentworth Higginson, who had been acquainted with the author and was familiar with some of her poems.

Higginson is the primary villain in most accounts of the editing of Emily Dickinson's poetry—a status that Thomas Johnson (who reedited Emily's poems in 1955 and finally brought about their publication in the versions she had actually written) has accounted for by calling Higginson, in his introduction, "a representative nineteenth-century traditionalist [who] was being asked to judge the work of a 'wholly new' order of craftsman...trying to measure a cube by the rules of plane geometry"—though I find things to praise in Higginson, if not exactly his editorial changes, and prefer to lay the blame more on the stifling Victorian middle-class conventionality-at-any-cost mindset of nineteenth-century America, and to illustrate this I would rather point to Arlo Bates, who (as the chief literary assistant to Thomas Niles, head man at Roberts Brothers publishers, whom Higginson had approached about Emily's poems) allowed as how the collection could be published, but only after a number of "absolutely necessary changes" were made, and on this particular matter I will give the final word to Thomas Johnson, who recognized that "Bates's suggestion about 'necessary' changes was no vagary. It was the established editorial procedure which had beset Emily Dickinson all her life; the kind that in fact had stiffened her determination never to let her verses be published. Death did not release her from the incubus of good intentions."

Shortly after the first selection of poems was published in 1890, Arlo Bates had this to say about them in the *Boston Courier:* "Had Miss Dickinson possessed the aptitude and the will to learn technical skill, she would have enriched the language with lyrics which would have endured to the end of time, it well might be. As it is, she has put upon paper things which will delight the few, but which will hold their place on sufferance, and as showing what she might have been rather than for what she was"—in response to which any undergraduate would be forgiven for sputtering, "I've heard of Emily Dickinson, but who in the name of Martha, Mary, and Little Baby Jesus is Arlo Bates?" though it would perhaps be better to let George Whicher do the talking: "In view of the ceaseless struggle between formalists and precisians, on the one hand, and the users of language for creative purposes, on the other, it may not be needless to insist that poetic power does not depend on conformity to grammar, logic, or any sort of mechanical correctness…We should not have much respect for a poet whose range of expression did not strain the capacities of everyday language, and we can have no respect at all for a critic who supposes that normal usage can be made into a yardstick for the measurement of poetic achievement"—particularly in view of the fact that the guy himself had recently been criticized for the similar difficulties that some saw in his prose style, in which often a whole paragraph will consist of but one extended sentence—compound, complex, and hopelessly complicated all at once—and indeed, whole essays by this guy consist of nothing but a sequence of such paragraphs made of such sentences, so help him God.

Certainly Thomas Wentworth Higginson was not the perfect reader for Emily Dickinson's poems, but in the preface he wrote for the 1890 selection, he actually seems to appreciate her unconventionality, for example when he says, "in many cases these verses will seem to the reader like poetry torn up by the roots, with rain and dew and earth still clinging to them, giving a freshness and a fragrance not otherwise to be conveyed," or when he recognizes that the reader will find here "flashes of wholly original and profound insight into nature and life; words and phrases exhibiting an extraordinary vividness of descriptive and imaginative power, yet often set in a seemingly whimsical or even rugged frame," or, finally, in the generosity of a comment in which he sums up his feelings by saying, "But the main quality of these poems is that of an extraordinary grasp and insight, uttered with an uneven vigor sometimes exasperating, seemingly wayward, but really unsought and inevitable," which, if Higginson had never changed a thing in her poems, would no doubt be quoted as one of the finest early comments on a difficult and wonderful poet. So Higginson's not so bad.

Birds and Bees and Silver Seas

Still, Higginson had his limitations, one of which was an inability to conceive that sexuality in any form, including the imaginative, could inhabit Emily Dickinson's mind, which I think is why, in a letter written to his coeditor, Mabel Loomis Todd, he reacted as he did to Emily's famously sexual poem, number 249—the one in which she longs for "Wild Nights—Wild Nights! / Were I with thee / Wild nights should be / Our luxury!"—of which he lamented, "One poem only I dread a little to print—that wonderful 'Wild Nights,'—lest the malignant read into it more than that virgin recluse ever dreamed of putting there," though certainly one need not be terribly malignant to see this poem as a simple precursor to a song by the Beach Boys (coalescers of so much of the wisdom of earlier American thinking and literature), "Wouldn't It Be Nice," in which the probably-not-so-virgin teenage boy speaker/singer fantasizes about the delicious time he and his girlfriend will have when they can finally cuddle together all night long, rather than merely up until the time of her curfew, and one can hardly read Emily's poem without thinking that she knew exactly whatof she spoke.

In accord with Higginson's wish, poem 249 did not appear in the first selection, issued in 1890, but did in the second, issued in 1891, an illustration perhaps of the powers of Mabel Loomis Todd—about whose own sexuality I shall have more to say presently—though the 1890 compilation did contain at least one poem, number 211, recognized by some twentieth-century critic, whose name the guy who married the insurance woman has forgotten to write down, as "openly erotic," and the guy certainly agrees, while further thinking the poem is so blatantly sexual as to have fooled Higginson into thinking it was innocently about flowers and gardens and bees, though certainly Mabel would not have been fooled—

Come slowly—Eden!
Lips unused to Thee—
Bashful—sip thy Jessamines—
As the fainting Bee—

Reaching late his flower,
Round her chamber hums—
Counts his nectars—
Enters—and is lost in Balms.—

which sounds Lewinskian in its first stanza, but decidedly copularlian in its second—and reading which the guy felt he had to conclude that its author knew once again, and intimately as it were, whatof she spoke, and he maintains that view to this day, though it is not one universally accepted by other readers and critics and writers.

Emily Dickinson may well have wanted to look like a sequestered virgin in the eyes of Thomas Wentworth Higginson, but the guy found himself suspecting that she probably knew other ways to appear, for indeed she wrote a great many love poems, which one of her best and most recent readers, Judith Farr (in her book *The Passion of Emily Dickinson*) divides into two groups, one of poems written to Samuel Bowles and the other of poems written to Sue Gilbert Dickinson, thereby suggesting but without ever exactly saying so that Emily's sexuality may have been, shall we say, bipolar; and Richard B. Sewell, Emily's biographer, tells the interesting story of the passionate and doubly adulterous affair carried on by Edward Dickinson, treasurer of the college, and Mabel Loomis Todd, wife of the college's biology professor, in the home of Emily and Lavinia, who surely were coconspirators with the lovers and helped them keep their secret from Sue, who figured it out anyway, to the detriment of her relationships with both Emily and Lavinia, to say nothing of her relationships with Mabel and Edward, with the wonderfully juicy detail that, in their great passion, they—Mabel and Edward—did *it* everywhere, including at least once on the dining room table.

I am suggesting, with the assistance of my friend the guy, that Emily Dickinson may have been a lively babe indeed, and the two of us think this is proved conclusively by a careful reading of her seldom-noticed poem number 520—

I started Early—Took my Dog—
And visited the Sea—
The Mermaids in the Basement
Came out to look at me—

And Frigates—in the Upper Floor
Extended Hempen Hands—
Presuming Me to be a Mouse—
Aground—upon the Sands—

But no Man moved Me—till the Tide
Went past my simple Shoe—
And past my Apron—and my Belt
And past my Boddice—too—

And made as He would eat me up—
As wholly as a Dew
Upon a Dandelion's Sleeve—
And then—I started—too—

And He—he followed—close behind—
I felt His Silver Heel
Upon my Ancle—Then my Shoes [sic]
Would overflow with Pearl—

Until We met the Solid Town—
No One He seemed to know—
And bowing—with a Mighty look—
At me—The Sea withdrew—

which has been noticed by only a few critics (not includ-ing the otherwise estimable Judith Farr), none of whom has quite been able to perceive its directness, its tricki-ness, and its simplicity—the comments range from Lau-rence Perrine's sober insistence that "the poet is describ-ing a morning walk to the sea," through George Whicher's oddly (for him) shallow thought that the poem is purely fanciful and humorous, Yvor Winters's typically abrupt in-sistence that it is about death, Kate Flores's rather warmer feeling that it is somehow about love, and Eric Carlson's hands-off belief that the poem is "a dramatization of the frightening realization that toying with love may arouse a tide of emotion too powerful to control," to John B. Pick-ard's still tame but welcome recognition of the poem's "mild sexual imagery" and his disappointing conclusion that "the basic theme is the rejection of one of life's prime forces—love, sex, beauty, or death—for a weak, conven-tional existence."

Emily Dickinson's poetry, like her life, is anything but weak and conventional, though appearances often indicate otherwise—for example, in her almost unvary-ing reliance on an approximation of the simplistic met-rical and rhyming form used in the standard hymns of her day, and in the way she misleads her readers about her real subject at the beginnings of so many of her po-ems, which is indeed the case in poem 520, the first two stanzas of which are so ridiculously unreal and playful that we must conclude that the real experience of the poem begins only with the shockingly direct word "Man" at the beginning of the third stanza, and from then on its implications ought to be perfectly clear, even though some critics have mistakenly thought the word "started" refers to the beginning of the speaker's flight away from her partner rather than to her surprise at the powerful and perhaps unfamiliar rush of feeling by which she is overcome, while others have mistakenly thought her mention of shoes overflowing with "Pearl" refers to the gems from which necklaces are made rather than, and I blush, to a liquid substance indicative of the achievement of sexual ecstacy.

The weak and conventional view of Emily Dickinson as a demure, spinsterly, virginal recluse is undoubtedly comforting to those who, despite their heroic misappropriations of Robert Frost's famous poem, are actually committed not to doing things differently but to preserving the social order of the status quo—with its richly developed sense of decorum, propriety, good manners, good grooming, and silence in the face of great passion—but this view is a fiction, a fiction created by persons who know too little about what really goes on in the hearts and minds of real writers, great writers, writers of deep and authentic feeling, writers such as Emily Dickinson, Robert Frost, Edgar Allan Poe, Wallace Stevens, and Jane Austen, none of whom was afraid to take the road unknown.

⤳ Edgar Allan Poe's Secret Sharer

I am certain that I bought these books from Melvin Mc-Cosh at his used bookstore in Minneapolis, in about 1962 or '63. I am certain that I found them on the fifth or sixth shelf up from the bottom, on the right-hand side of the left-hand aisle, about halfway between the door and McCosh's desk. Three compact volumes, bound in one-quarter leather, with marbled boards, endpapers, and edges, measuring about five by seven and a half inches, the pages trimmed on all four sides and sewn straight through from front to back rather than trimmed on two or three sides and sewn, section by section, through the folds on the fourth side, with the sections then gathered and tied together, using these same threads. There are terms for these things, and I ought to know them, but I don't. I loved the look of these books, loved how old they were; I had read with admiration nearly all of the author's tales when I was still in high school; I was now a serious student of literature and could afford the seven dollars and fifty cents. But it was not until many years later that I learned the significance of what I had purchased: "*The Works of the Late Edgar Allan Poe*, with a Memoir by Rufus

Wilmot Griswold and Notices of His Life and Genius by N. P. Willis and J. R. Lowell."

Here is what I eventually found out: Shortly before his death, Poe had told Muddy—Maria Clemm, his beloved aunt and mother-in-law—that he wanted Rufus Wilmot Griswold—not only Poe's bitterest enemy but one of the nastiest men in America—to act as his literary executor. Poe knew that he and Griswold were not friends—indeed, they had been snarling at one another for years—but he must have assumed (as he so often did) that truth would be served in spite of human vagary, that literature would win out in the end. And he was right, in a way: literature did win out, and Poe is listed among the great American writers. But he is not listed among the great American men; he is not generally thought of even as a good man, and that is thanks largely to the Reverend Rufus Wilmot Griswold. Through the many lies that he told after Poe's death, Griswold did everything he could to destroy Poe's reputation, then and forever.

Griswold was a logical choice. Despite his nastiness, perhaps because of it, he was probably the best-known editorial hack of his day, and a collected edition prepared by him was likely to sell well. The profits would go to Muddy, as Poe's heir, and Muddy needed money; like Poe, Muddy always needed money. Poe died on the seventh of October, 1849, and Griswold's edition of the *Works*, with his infamous "Memoir" placed at the beginning of the third volume, was published in 1850. In my set, printed in 1853, the memoir is placed at the start of the first volume, and volume three begins on page twenty-one. I could tell you a lot of other things about these idiosyncratic books (for example, most of the sections are twenty-four pages long, an uncommon number, while the last section of the first volume is only two pages long, one sheet of paper, and in my set it is bound upside down), but what really interests me is Rufus Wilmot Griswold and his vicious memoir.

Though Griswold is relatively fair when commenting on Poe's work, he fabricates lie after lie when talking about Poe's behavior, character, and reputation. In *The Poe Log* (1987)—a chronological compendium of facts relating to Poe—Dwight Thomas and David K. Jackson call the memoir "malicious and false," and say that "For several decades [it] served as the standard biography of Poe [and] has had a lasting influence on the popular conception of his personality." How well Griswold succeeded in his assassination of Poe's character may be gleaned from a comment first published in the *Edinburgh Review* in 1858, then reprinted elsewhere in the United Kingdom:

> Edgar Allan Poe was incontestably one of the most worthless persons of whom we have any record in the world of letters . . . He outraged his benefactor, he deceived his friends, he sacrificed his love, he became a beggar, a vagabond, the slanderer of a woman, the delirious drunken pauper of a common hospital, hated by some, despised by others, and avoided by all respectable men.

Certainly Poe had his faults—he was a human being, after all—but the notion of him as a worthless, outrageous, hated slanderer of women, as the deceiving, delirious, drunken, despised beggar who "sacrificed his love"—his beloved wife Virginia!—is a myth created by Rufus Griswold.

Among the other lies that Griswold tells in his memoir are these: that Poe was expelled from the University of Virginia for dissipation; that he deserted his post with the United States Army; that he won the *Saturday Visiter* award for best tale ("MS Found in a Bottle") only because one of the judges happened to admire Poe's handwriting and so "Not another ms was unfolded"; that he attempted to seduce his foster father's second wife; that he said to one of his good friends, "Burton, I am—*the editor—of the Penn Magazine*—and you are—hiccup—*a fool*"; that "some of his plagiarisms are scarcely paralleled for their audacity in all literary history"; that he slept with ("had criminal relations with") Muddy. None of this is true. But because these lies were told by the dead writer's literary executor, most readers accepted them at face value, and most still do.

Worse perhaps than these outright fabrications are Griswold's more quietly sinister touches—his silent revisions of Poe's letters; his smug sense of moral superiority; his insidious asides; his nasty, condescending tone. Poe's letters still exist, so it is possible to compare the versions Griswold printed with the originals. Here, for example, is the letter that Poe wrote Griswold on February 24, 1845; I have italicized the sentences that Griswold added to Poe's actual text:

A thousand thanks for your kindness in the matter of those books, which I could not afford to buy, and had so much need of. Soon after seeing you, I sent you, through Zieber, all my poems worth republishing, and I presume they reached you. *I was sincerely delighted with what you said of them, and if you will write your criticism in the form of a preface, I shall be greatly obliged to you. I say this not because you praised me: everybody praises me now: but because you so perfectly understand me, or what I have aimed at, in all my poems: I did not think you had so much delicacy of appreciation joined with your strong sense; I can say that no man's approbation gives me so much pleasure.* I send you with this another package, also through Zieber, by Burgess & Stringer. It contains, in the way of essay, "Mesmeric Revelation," which I would like to have go in, even if you have to omit the "House of Usher." I send also corrected copies of (in the way of funny criticism, but you don't like this) "Flaccus," which conveys a tolerable idea of my style; and of my serious manner "Barnaby Rudge" is a good specimen. In the tale line, "The Murders of the Rue Morgue," "The Gold Bug," and "The Man that was Used Up,"—far more than enough, but you can select to suit yourself. I prefer the "G. B." to the "M. in the R. M." I have taken a third interest in the "Broadway Journal," and will be glad if you could send me anything for it. *Why not let me anticipate the book publication of your splendid essay on Milton?*

Poe's own words are cool and professional; Griswold has asked him what he would like included in a new anthology, and Poe answers. At the end he does Griswold the favor of asking him to submit something to Poe's own new magazine. But he does not praise Griswold's pedestrian essay on Milton; he does not thank Griswold for his nonexistent act of charity; he does not confess his own poverty; he does not brag that everyone praises him; he does not salute Griswold as the most brilliant of all his critics. Griswold's additions to the letter are breathtakingly self-serving and sinister. He has Poe condemn himself in words he never wrote; he has Poe praise from beyond the grave the generosity, goodness, and brilliance of the very man who is enacting his, Poe's, moral execution. No wonder Max J. Hertzberg, editor of *The Reader's Encyclopedia of American Literature,* called Griswold "the worst liar and the least likable man in the whole history of American literature."

LET ME TELL YOU THE WORST THINGS I KNOW ABOUT Edgar Allan Poe. He was arrogant, demanding, and irresponsible. Although he had a wife and mother-in-law to support, he could not, perhaps would not, hold a job. As a critic and editor he occasionally praised unworthy writers (including Rufus Griswold) as a way of enhancing his career. Late in his life, after the death of Virginia, he pursued a series of wealthy widows hoping to find a wife to support him and Muddy (she was his father's sister; after Virginia's death, he continued to live with her; he addressed her as "Mother"). He shamelessly asked people—friends, business associates, mere acquaintances—for money, and he did not always repay their loans. He sometimes drank to excess and disappeared for days at a time; occasionally he ended up in jail or in a hospital or walking the gutters of some other town. But he did not copy other people's works and try to pass them off as his own, though he echoed phrases in making his own poems; he imported ideas but used them to his own ends. All writers do these things—some more, and more skillfully, than others. T. S. Eliot understood this better than Griswold ever did: "Immature poets imitate; mature poets steal." In other words, Poe was neither a saint nor a monster. And there are compelling reasons for much of his behavior, at least in the eyes of persons for whom propriety is not life's highest virtue.

Here is the truth about Poe's childhood. His biological parents lived a hand-to-mouth existence as actors in a traveling troupe; when Edgar was nine months old, his father abandoned the family—to this day, no one knows what became of him. Two years later Edgar watched as his mother, Eliza, became ill, declined precipitously, and died. She was a beautiful woman, a talented actress, youthful in age and appearance: her hair was full and dark; her eyes were hauntingly large and dark; she was Ligeia, she was Annabel Lee, she was Lenore. And because of the itinerant nature of the family's life, she was everything to Edgar; his dependence on her was complete. I don't imagine that the three-year-old Poe was "thinking" much of anything as he gazed upon her lifeless body in that tawdry rooming house in Richmond, but certainly the pattern for his whole life was on display for him there.

Almost immediately, in what looks like a rare stroke of good luck, he was taken in by a wealthy young couple, John and Fanny Allan. A generous and loving woman, Fanny was beautiful, with dark hair and large eyes. Unfortunately, her husband was a niggardly and resentful man. He had been unloved as a child, had been given nothing, and he was damned if he was going to behave any differently to his wife's ragged orphan. In the words of Kenneth Silverman, Poe's most recent and best biographer, Allan "despised dependence," but his "code of independence [had] a begrudging, envious quality. His 'Stand on your own two feet' ever registered 'Why should you get what I did not?'" He began by refusing to adopt the child. Though she truly loved Edgar, Fanny could not overcome the cruelty of her husband; besides resembling Poe's birth mother in her looks, she resembled her also in being frail, defenseless. Griswold's glib account of Poe's childhood paints the worst possible picture while ignoring the true history of conflict and eventual defeat: "The proud, nervous irritability of the boy's nature was fostered by his guardian's well-meant but ill-judged indulgence. Nothing was permitted which could 'break his spirit.' He must be the master of his masters, or not have any."

As time went by, Fanny's perpetual state of illness (a second fading mother) made her increasingly unavailable to Edgar. He seems to have gravitated toward other motherly women, in particular, when he was about fourteen, to Mrs. Jane Stanard, the mother of one of his schoolmates. But she too was sickly (a third fading mother), and she died soon after, at the age of thirty-one. When Poe fell into the habit of visiting her grave, John Allan became irritated; Allan was always irritated, always doing nasty little things to his ward. He was proud of the education he gave Poe, for example, but he sent him to the University of Virginia with only enough money for tuition, nothing for books, nothing for room and board. Poe—a brilliant student—was forced to borrow some of the money he needed and tried gambling for the rest. When the year was over, he arrived home deep in debt. He and Allan quarreled, and Poe set off on his own. While he was gone Fanny died, on the twenty-eighth of February, 1829, at the age of forty-four. Over the next five years, the gulf between Poe and John Allan continued to widen; though Poe reached out several times, Allan generally responded with contempt. He did not approve of Poe's love of literature and seems in general to have viewed him as a moral leper. By the time Allan died in 1834, he would not so much as speak Poe's name; his entire fortune went to his young second wife.

Poe moved to Baltimore in 1831 and, desperate for the love family could provide, soon was living with Muddy and her nine-year-old daughter Virginia. Poe and Virginia married in 1835, and in January of 1842, while singing, she suddenly began to cough up blood. This was the first sign of the tuberculosis that kept her seriously ill for the next four years and caused her death in November 1846. In marrying his thirteen-year-old cousin, Poe was certainly violating the standards of propriety, but there is no indication anywhere that he was motivated by anything other than love and spiritual longing, a deep emotional hunger. Between the two of them, Muddy and Virginia filled the void left in Poe's heart by the death of his mother. Virginia was young and sickly, with dark eyes and dark hair; Muddy was maternal and practical. The arrangement was unusual, but Poe was an unusual man with unusual needs: haunted, haggard, hungry, and bereaved; impoverished, unsettled, forsaken, and betrayed.

Just how deeply Virginia resembled Eliza is evident in a passage from George Graham's reminiscence of Poe (Graham was the publisher of *Graham's Magazine* and Poe's employer for a time):

> His love for his wife was a sort of rapturous worship of the spirit of beauty which he felt was fading before his eyes. I have seen him hovering around her when she was ill, with all the fond fear and anxiety of a mother for her first-born—her slightest cough causing in him a shudder, a heart-chill that was visible. I rode out one summer evening with them, and the remembrance of his watchful eyes eagerly bent upon the slightest change of hue in that loved face, haunts me yet as the memory of a sad strain.

How few people in any age have the wisdom to understand anything subtle, we know; how few people in any age have the wisdom to understand with sympathy the dark subtleties of the human heart, we also know. But the nineteenth century, the century of Queen Victoria, was an unusually prudish time, in America as in England, and Rufus Griswold was more than just a man of his time. As we shall see, he had his own dark subtleties . . .

Does there not exist in America an ordinance which forbids to curs an entrance to the cemeteries?

—Charles Baudelaire, on Rufus Griswold's
treatment of Edgar Poe

Following the death of Edgar Allan Poe at the age of forty in 1849, Muddy, perhaps in accordance with Poe's wishes, asked the Reverend Rufus Wilmot Griswold to serve as Poe's literary executor. Griswold was an unfortunate choice. Even before being approached by Muddy, Griswold had written a slanderous obituary notice on Poe, using the pen-name Ludwig, for Horace Greeley's *New York Tribune.* When he issued *The Works of Edgar Allan Poe,* Griswold incorporated his obituary into the much longer and equally nasty "Memoir" that he wrote for the collection. That Griswold disliked Poe is not surprising, given the bickering that went on between the two for the whole eight years of their acquaintance. Poe didn't like Griswold either, though he was goodhearted enough (naive enough, foolish enough) to trust him. But mere bickering will not explain the depth of Griswold's viciousness; to understand that we are going to have to take a close look at his character and his career. We are going to have to compare Rufus Griswold to the man—to the writer and editor, the husband, nephew, and son—whose character and reputation he tried to destroy. What makes Poe so unusual among the best American writers is the complexity of his mind, his strength not just of imagination (which is dominant in his tales and poems) but also of analytical intellect (dominant in his stories and literary criticism).

Probably because Poe, at the age of two, had to watch

his mother slowly decline and die of consumption, his tales and poems are saturated with metaphysical questions: the nature of time and eternity; the nature of death and its relationship to life; the possibilities of life after death. These works are doubly haunted—on their surfaces by the dead and dying, at their depths by a complex mingling of desire and fear, for love and for death, for the self and for the dead beloved. Poe was well aware that his obsession with death, like the bizarre schemes for resurrecting the dead incorporated into some of his tales, may have been based more on the subjective projections of a disordered mind than on the objective perceptions of a clear-seeing intellect. Thus his tales and poems are not just creatively and metaphysically profound, they are psychologically profound as well. Though primarily dominated by imagination, these works are also informed by the analytical intellect.

The balance is reversed in Poe's stories (a tale is a work of romance, a work of convoluted and patterned imagination; a story is a more objective work of narration) and literary criticism. Poe invented the detective story, in which a brilliant investigator uses a version of the scientific method to solve a mystery so complicated that even the most attentive reader is likely to remain stumped until the end, as is the case in "The Murders in the Rue Morgue" and "The Gold Bug." Such writers as Arthur Conan Doyle, Agatha Christie, Nero Wolfe, P. D. James, and Ruth Rendell owe their very genre to the genius of Edgar Allan Poe. His literary criticism is equally analytical, as George Snell makes clear in contrasting Poe's practice to that of James Russell Lowell:

Compared to Lowell's criticism, nothing more than leisurely "studies" in taste, Poe's is like a knife laying bare the sinews and nerves of the work under review. From Lowell one may get an impression of life interpreted through literature, of historical tangents, of wide philosophical generalizations; but this is merely impressionistic. From Poe we learn how the writer wrote as he has written, how he has used or failed to use the techniques available.

Poe was concerned with the craft, the artistry, the construction of the work rather than merely with its content and ideas; he believed a work of art should *affect* its readers or viewers, not teach them; it must not be didactic.

Above all it should not be morally didactic, it should not preach; its tendency toward goodness, if any, should be implicit, not explicit. As Snell has also pointed out, Poe's abhorrence of moral didacticism is the cause of much of the enmity that has been directed against him, in his day and after:

Poe's opposition to didacticism in poetry and fiction has occasioned charges from some quarters that he was, at bottom, little concerned with ethics, and that as a result the tendency of his work was not moral... The truth is, Poe never wrote a line that could be construed as inciting to a breakdown of morality. What he stood most vigorously against was simply the moralizing of a Longfellow, or the didactic intent in Wordsworth. A work of art should be nothing but itself—should have no ulterior aim.

Poe questioned these writers, that is, for their literary practice, not for their moral values. Unfortunately, Poe lived during the age of Queen Victoria, a time of intense moralism—by which I mean not true morality, but propriety, the *appearance* of morality—in America as in England. Thus Poe was open to the condemnation of his smaller-minded literary contemporaries, who suspected him of being an evil man because he did not want Henry Wadsworth Longfellow telling him, in poems, how to live his life.

Rufus Griswold played this game, with Poe and many other writers, but he was not a small-minded man. Nor was he encumbered by a highly developed moral sense. Intelligent, cunning, ambitious, and blithely hypocritical, Griswold was willing to do just about anything in order to promote his own career and elevate himself above writers who were in reality much superior to him. Because of the moralism of the age, he was happy to pretend to be a moralist, if it would sell his books. Thus we find his twentieth-century biographer, Joy Bayless, characterizing Griswold's introduction to his anthology *Poets and Poetry of America* in this fashion: "He rejoiced in the moral purity of the poetry that had been produced, pointing out that 'nearly everything in the poetic manner produced in this country is free from licentiousness, and harmless, if not elevating in its tendencies.'" We can all sleep better, knowing this.

Though he did try his hand at poetry, none of Griswold's creative writings is of the slightest interest today. Similarly, his criticism—because it is so baldly, so calculatedly self-serving—is of virtually no value. Primarily, Griswold was an anthologist, a compiler of the work of other writers. He produced dozens of anthologies on almost every conceivable subject, to the point where he was roundly mocked in the newspapers of the day. Here is one such comment:

> The Reverend Dr. Ridiculous W. Grizwold is in town superintending the publication of his great work, "The Advertisers and the Advertisements of America"... The volume is to be illustrated by a bouquet of heads, done in brass, of those who have acquired fame in this high branch of scholastic composition. This latest work, it is said, will be the author's greatest. Would it not be desirable that this greatest should be his last?

The comment was published on the seventh of June, 1845, well before Griswold had even hit his stride. Among the more notable anthologies that he produced are *The Poetry of Sentiments, The Poetry of Love, The Poetry of Flowers, The Poetry of Passions,* and *The Poetry of Affections.*

GRISWOLD AND POE MET IN MAY OF 1841, IN PHILADELphia. Poe was editing *Graham's Magazine* and Griswold was working for a newspaper while compiling *The Poets and Poetry of America,* which would be published the next year. The two men spent an afternoon together, no doubt talking about the literary world in general and their own particular projects. Griswold asked Poe to send him some poems for the anthology, and Poe agreed to do so. Everything seemed to have gone well; certainly Edgar thought that it had.

Almost immediately, however, something strange happened. Poe wrote a negative review of the poetry of Charles Sprague, a Boston banker, and published it in *Graham's*. A month later he wrote and published a review containing some mild praise of Pliny Earle, a physician-poet living in Philadelphia. By then Griswold himself had moved to Boston, and there he published a reply to Poe. He declared Sprague's poetry to be brilliant, "inimitable," and said of Pliny Earle: "We have been called upon in our time to examine vast quantities of rant and puerility, with which inexperienced boys or weak-minded men have attempted to win popular admiration; but we never saw anything more ineffably senseless and bombastic, than these verses so lauded by the editor of *Graham's Magazine*." By the time Griswold wrote these words, he had met Sprague and identified him as one of the five foremost poets living in America; the other four were Longfellow, William Cullen Bryant, Fitz-Greene Halleck, and Richard Henry Dana.

It is possible that Poe never saw this review by Griswold; but early in 1842, three additional events took place that would be of crucial importance in the developing relationship of the two men: Griswold's anthology was published, Poe left his job at *Graham's*, and Griswold was hired to replace Poe at *Graham's*. Almost immediately Griswold began criticizing his predecessor. When a reviewer for the *Independent,* published in Washington, D.C., gushed that Griswold's anthology was a work of "genius," an anonymous correspondent replied: "Mr. Griswold is a lively and elegant writer of prose and poetry, and a very fair and impartial critic, though the sponsor, as editor of *Graham's Magazine,* of the malignant, unjust, and disgraceful attacks on the literary character of its former editor, Mr. Poe."

In one hundred fifty-six years, no one has come up with a solid reason to explain why Griswold turned so quickly against Poe after their seemingly friendly first meeting—though we do know that it would not have taken much to set him off. A "friendly acquaintance" of Griswold's described him as generous, capable of "acts of kindness," but also as "one of the most irritable and vindictive men I ever met, if he fancied he was in any way familiarly treated,—when he became savage." Had Poe somehow treated Griswold "familiarly" during their meeting, perhaps by flattering him, but then not following up on the flattery? Had he questioned some aspect of the planned anthology, perhaps Griswold's curious overestimation of Sprague, Halleck, and Dana? Or had Poe not treated Griswold familiarly *enough*?

At first hearing, this last possibility sounds absurd, but Kenneth Silverman points out a pattern that makes it more credible: "Restless and rebellious as a youth, [Griswold] formed a habit of close but short-lived attachments, some of them with men slightly older than himself." (Poe was six years older than Griswold, and considerably more advanced in his career.) When Griswold was about sixteen years old, he ran away from his home near Orwell,

Vermont, to the big city of Albany, where he shared a room with a musician and journalist named George "Gaslight" Foster. After Griswold left suddenly a year later, Foster wrote him a letter:

> I have loved often and deeply. My heart has burned itself almost to a charred cinder by the flames of passion which have glowed within it—and yet I never felt towards any human being—man or woman—so strong and absorbing an affection as I bear to you.

The letter ends, "Farewell—Farewell—come to me if you love me." Griswold never went back, but he "preserved the letter until his death."

It does seem possible that Griswold was homosexual or bisexual, but I think it is unlikely. What we see instead is an unequal pattern in his intimate relationships; though others were willing to give their affections freely to Griswold, he was not able to give his affections to them. He abandoned Foster abruptly after living with him for a year. Similarly, he lived with his first wife, Carolyn Searles, for only about a year, then left her in New York to pursue his career elsewhere. He returned only occasionally, to visit her and their two children. When she suddenly died, Griswold made an extravagant display of grief at her funeral, then spent the whole night alone in her tomb, supposedly cradling her head in his arms and weeping into her hair.

Carolyn was from a wealthy family; Griswold's second wife was an heiress, wealthy on her own. Though he would have preferred to marry a friend of hers, Griswold settled for Charlotte Myers when the friend turned him down. Given the coolness he showed toward her, it seems obvious that Griswold married Charlotte for her money and the comfortable life he thought she would give him. Not long after the wedding, he declared her "incapable of being a wife" and filed for divorce. Precisely what he meant, again no one knows. Charlotte did take Griswold's daughter Caroline into her home, however, and seems to have been an excellent stepmother to her, even after they both had been abandoned by Griswold. As time went by, Caroline increasingly refused to have anything to do with her father, and when he died she did not attend his funeral.

Griswold's third and final wife, Harriet McCrillis, was also a wealthy woman in her own right, and Griswold seems to have had his best relationship with her. They married but maintained separate residences. A year before his death, she left him in New York and returned to her family home in Maine. She never spoke with or wrote to him again, and she did not attend his funeral. When asked about Rufus, she described him as a minor event in a long and mostly pleasant life. Once again we don't know exactly what came between them.

The pattern of these relationships suggests strongly that, while Griswold was unable to care for others, he needed, perhaps demanded, adoration from them. To a man like Gaslight Foster, Griswold perhaps seemed a mental giant. But Poe was on another level altogether, smart enough to know how smart he himself was. Though he was willing to be friendly to Griswold, he would not—could not—worship him as Griswold (who perhaps was just stupid enough not to know that he was stupid) demanded. But alas, hell hath no fury like a vain man scorned. The option Griswold seems always to have turned to was a cold vengeance, a calculating hatred. Griswold hated Poe deeply and pathologically, hated him as such a man could only hate someone he actually loved, hated him forever and beyond the grave.

POE'S NEEDS WERE AT LEAST AS GREAT AS GRISWOLD'S, BUT his close relationships followed a different pattern. Poe's hunger was not for blind adoration, but for the love of his dead mother: "I have many occasional dealings with Adversity," he said late in life, "but the want of parental affection has been the heaviest of my trials." Just how heavy the burden was may be gauged from something the British writer Somerset Maugham said, shortly before his death. As Maugham's nephew told the story, the two were sitting by the fire after dinner, reminiscing, when Maugham grew quiet. After a minute or two he muttered, seemingly out of the blue, "I shall never get over her death. I shall never get over it." The nephew assumed Maugham was talking about his wife, but gradually realized that the author was in fact talking about his mother, who had died more than eighty years earlier, when Maugham was only eight years old.

Poe spent his whole life searching for someone to replace his mother. Fanny Allan might have filled this role, but her husband would not allow it; she was also sickly and died well before her time, leaving Edgar once more alone. When Poe attached himself to Muddy soon thereafter, he was obviously looking again for his mother. Oddly, he was doing the same thing, though in quite a different way, when he married her thirteen-year-old daughter, Virginia. "Sissy," as he called Virginia, had more than a superficial resemblance to Poe's actual mother, Eliza: both were young, thin, and sickly; both had dark hair and soulful eyes; both eventually died from consumption.

In his great loneliness following the death of Virginia, Poe tried to replace her by pursuing a series of women. While this was going on, he and Muddy were close friends with a neighbor of theirs in Fordham, New York, a woman named Loui Shew. A nurse and student of literature, Loui possessed an unusual understanding of both human feelings and the medical implications inherent in them. She cared for Poe during some of his hardest times; she counseled him and ministered to him. Eventually she decided she had to wean him from her. According to Silverman, she "told [Poe] candidly that nothing could prevent his sudden death but a calmly prudent life, with a woman fond and strong enough to manage his affairs in his best interest." Poe agreed with the wisdom of what she said, but knew that her loss "was a fearful one ... unless some true and tender and pure womanly love saves me, I shall hardly last a year longer, alone."

Despite the accusations of Rufus Griswold—that Poe tried to seduce John Allan's second wife, that he had sex with Muddy, that he behaved improperly toward Mrs. Sarah Whitman and other women—Poe seems to have been almost prudish about sex. Elizabeth Oakes Smith, a contemporary novelist who knew Poe well, felt that "generally the bent of his feelings so far as women were concerned were totally of an ideal kind." Silverman similarly speaks of Poe's "moral primness and complex aversion to at least undomesticated sex," and concludes: "Far from challenging cultural norms, Poe in many tales and poems delineated in a transmuted form the culturally feminine values endorsed in the sickliest sentimental fiction of his day, upholding them much as he did in his own life."

As for Poe's relationship with Muddy, I think it is best summed up by the last words he spoke to her. About to board his train, Poe turned to Muddy and said, as she recalled: "God bless my own darling Muddy do not fear for your Eddy see how good I will be while I am away from you, and will come back to love and comfort you." The reason Poe worried so much about money for most of his adult life was because he felt obligated to support Muddy and Sissy. The love he expresses here is ideal indeed, the sort of love that you, dear reader (dear writer), may have expressed for your dying father as you gave him his shot of morphine and wiped the perspiration from his brow.

POE HAD AN EXTREMELY DIFFICULT LIFE, AND NOT ALL his troubles had to do with women. Though he is also generally thought to have been an ill-mannered drunk, charitably an alcoholic, Poe's actual problem was that his body could not tolerate alcohol. Any amount was too much for him, as Muddy said; after one or two glasses of wine, "he was not responsible for either his words, or actions." When Poe drank he would become arrogant and abusive; he would lose his possessions, his shirt, his shoes, his luggage, his wallet; he would be unable to find his way home.

The obvious question—why did this man drink?—is almost insulting: he was a human being, not an automaton, and he had good reasons for wanting to escape from the harsh realities of his life. More specifically, when his friend George Eveleth asked Poe about his spells of drinking and insanity, Poe attributed them to his agony over the long illness and death of Sissy: "... at each accession of the disorder I loved her more dearly & clung to her life with more desperate pertinacity. I became insane, with long intervals of horrible sanity. During these fits of absolute unconsciousness I drank, God only knows how often or how much. As a matter of course, my enemies referred the insanity to the drink rather than the drink to the insanity." Certainly Poe knew that drinking would not solve his problems; but (big surprise) he drank anyway.

Poe's other major problem was money. He was a great writer but only occasionally a popular writer; he never wrote anything like a best seller. He was a brilliant editor, but the demands of such a job interfered seriously with his need to write. In spite of all of his troubles, however, and in spite of his increasingly bad health, Poe worked on—heroically, we might conclude, as did Kenneth Silverman:

> It would seem that only by some defiantly willed self-transcendence could he produce so many works of such vast popularity and influence in between his hard-up wanderings from home to home and job to job, insulting friends or not pay-

ing the barber when lost in bourbon and port, so distressed by Virginia's hemorrhaging that he could not speak of it, not to mention the wave of disaster and affront that began practically with his birth.

Far from being the libertine we read of in Griswold's "Memoir," Poe was a victim, horribly a victim—first of life and then of Rufus Griswold.

APPARENTLY GRISWOLD BEGAN SNIPING AT POE ALMOST immediately after their first meeting; Poe's response, if response it was, came several months later. In Philadelphia on November 21, 1843, and in other cities, Poe criticized Griswold's anthology during his lecture on "American Poetry." Although the text of the lecture does not survive, it was described in newspapers: Griswold's choices show a "miserable want of judgment"; he frequently presents the "worst specimens" of a good writer's work while giving "an extravagant proportion of space" to bad poets who were his close friends; for example, Gaslight Foster, Charles Sprague, and Charles Fenno Hoffman. When Poe realized that he had made a bad political blunder, he apologized to Griswold and promised not to misbehave again. But Poe was telling the truth: all of Griswold's anthologies are notably weak; he seems to have followed a personal agenda, or a strictly financial agenda, in compiling every one of them. By printing the lesser works of greater writers, he tried to lower them to his own level; by printing at all the works of a negligible writer but serious banker like Charles Sprague, he curried favor with the wealthy.

Poe, meanwhile, tried hard in his reviews and critical essays to tell the truth as he saw it, no matter the consequences. Certainly there were cases in which he compromised his values for personal reasons of one sort or another, but generally he was a man of high principle, whatever the cost. And the cost was high. James Wood Davidson has pointed out that Poe

> secured more and more *bitter* enemies than any other American author has done, because he told more wholesome truths than any other author has dared to tell. And if there is any one thing the exposition of which a man will not forgive, that thing is the truth. A slandered man may find repose beneath the shade of his real or imagined injuries, but the stern truth leaves no covert to flee to, save vengeance against the utterer.

Although Griswold pretended to accept Poe's apology, the damage had been done; Griswold was "a dangerous person to be connected with," as Ann Sophia Stephens, another contemporary novelist, said.

Perhaps Griswold, in his own criticism and in his memoir of Poe, also wanted only to speak the truth as he saw it. If so, then we would have to wonder why one of his earliest associates, a man who worked with him in Vermont in 1839, breathed a sigh of relief when Griswold left town, calling him "talented and industrious: but … too d——d unscrupulous." Similarly, Griswold's early friends in New York would sometimes ask—laughingly, admiringly, nervously—"Is that a Griswold or a fact?" Griswold's literary relationships held up no better than his personal relationships. For much of his life, he was a protégé of Horace Greeley and worked on many of Greeley's newspapers. But when Griswold died, Greeley did not attend the funeral; when he wrote his voluminous memoirs, Greeley did not mention Griswold's name.

The scope of Griswold's vindictiveness, dishonesty, and disloyalty is clearly on display in the preface of his memoir, in which he answers the many friends and associates of Poe who had objected in public to the obituary that Griswold had earlier published under the pseudonym Ludwig. He begins by explaining that "my unconsidered and imperfect, but as every one who knew its subject readily perceived, very kind article, was now vehemently attacked." One of the attackers was George Rex Graham, who, as owner and publisher of *Graham's Magazine*, had generously employed both Griswold and Poe. In his rebuttal, Griswold characterizes his former employer as "this silly and ambitious person" and the letter he wrote as "sophomorical and trashy." He does not even grant Graham his personhood, beginning "A writer under the signature of 'George R. Graham.'" Of another of his critics, Griswold says: "Mr. John Neal, too, who had never had even the slightest personal acquaintance with Poe in his life [a transparent lie], rushes from a sleep which the public had trusted was eternal, to declare that my characterization of Poe . . . is false and malicious, and that I am a 'caluminator,' a 'Rhadamanthus,' etc."

Perhaps the oddest aspect of the Griswold–Poe relationship shows up in Griswold's dealings with two of the women whom Poe had courted after the death of Virginia. Fanny Osgood, a poet, was another of Poe's Elizas, a beautiful, dark, sickly woman with soulful eyes. Near the end of the memoir, Griswold congratulates himself for "having, in no ungenerous spirit, presented the chief facts in Mr. Poe's history, not designedly exaggerating his genius [and] not bringing into bolder relief than was just and necessary his infirmities." He then claims to have received Mrs. Osgood's approval of his views: "she said she did not doubt that my view of Mr. Poe, which she knew indeed to be the common view, was perfectly just." Unfortunately, Fanny Osgood was dead by the time Griswold's memoir was published, so we will never know if she actually said this. What she wrote about Poe, however, still exists: "I can sincerely say, that although I have frequently *heard* of aberrations on his part from 'the straight and narrow path,' I have never seen him otherwise than gentle, generous, well-bred, and fastidiously refined ... there was a peculiar and irresistible charm in the chivalric, graceful, and almost tender reverence with which he invariably approached all women."

That Griswold tried to use Mrs. Osgood to further his own agenda is not surprising; what is very surprising, however, is something he said much earlier to Sarah "Helen" Whitman, during the time when Poe was pressing her to marry him. As Silverman tells the story, "When Helen asked [Griswold] why so many of the New York literati disliked Poe, he said Poe had done nothing 'exceptionally wrong' and was less blamable than his enemies for his literary embroilments." For once, at least, Griswold spoke the truth of Poe; spoke truer, perhaps, than he realized.

Perhaps the best assessment ever made of Griswold's

memoir appeared immediately after the publication of *The Works of Edgar Allan Poe.* Writing in the *Saturday Evening Post*, of which he was editor, Henry Peterson said: "Considering this biography as the work of a literary executor, we must say that a more cold-blooded and ungenerous composition has seldom come under our notice. Nothing so condemnatory of Mr. Poe, so absolutely blasting to his character has ever appeared in print... It is absolutely horrible (considering the circumstances under which Mr. Griswold writes) with what cool deliberateness he charges upon Mr. Poe the basest and most dishonorable actions."

The last meeting between Griswold and Poe took place at the very beginning of the last trip Poe took, just before his death, the trip before which he said his farewell to Muddy. Poe and Griswold met for dinner in New York, and afterward Poe—oddly, and in direct contradiction to what he had promised Muddy—went out and got drunk. Much later that night, he was found by friends and hospitalized with an irregular pulse. Clearly the meeting with Griswold had upset Poe, though, as usual, we have no idea why; Silverman speculates that "Something apparently stirred in Poe during dinner with Griswold, deep perhaps calling unto deep." Even when not in the upsetting presence of Griswold, Poe was both ill and deeply depressed at this time. In a journal note written sometime between April and July of 1849, Poe said "my sadness is unaccountable, and this makes me the more sad. *Nothing* cheers or comforts me. My life seems wasted—the future looks a dreary blank." At about the same time, Muddy wrote in a letter to Poe: "God knows I wish we were both in our graves, it would, I am sure, be far better." Finally, when Poe was breathing his last in the hospital in Baltimore, his doctor tried to console him by saying that his friends would arrive soon. In the words of the doctor: "At this he broke out with much energy and said the best thing his best friend could do would be to blow out his brains with a pistol." Poe's last words, as recorded by this same doctor, were: "Lord help my poor soul."

Griswold's last years were not much better. He had several accidents, some almost funny, some not. On one occasion, after he had finally succeeded in securing a contract for the publication of a book of Fanny Osgood's poems, Griswold fell from a ferry boat and almost drowned while rushing to tell her the news. Another time an explosion from a gas leak in his rented room caused him to be badly burned; he lost seven fingernails trying to fight the blaze. Even more seriously, Griswold, too, suffered from consumption and spent his last years gradually dying— "rarely leaving his rooms . . . [enduring] attacks of vertigo, sometimes crying, exhausted, scarcely caring to live, taking opium for energy to write." Finally, deserted by everyone to whom he had ever been close, Griswold died alone in a tawdry rented room in New York City. On his walls hung three portraits: one of himself, one of Fanny Osgood, and one of Edgar Allan Poe.

MY FAVORITE IRONY IN THIS STORY IS THAT THE PERFECT epitaph to Griswold's life may have been written, near the beginning of their association, by Poe. According to Joy

Bayless, these prophetic words appeared anonymously in a newspaper in 1843; she seems quite certain of their authorship:

> Forgotten, save only by those whom he has injured and insulted, he will sink into oblivion, without leaving a landmark to tell that he once existed; or, if he is spoken of hereafter, he will be quoted as the unfaithful servant who abused his trust.

Truer words have seldom been spoken: nothing written by Rufus Wilmot Griswold has stood the test of time; he is remembered today only for the vile and faithless memoir he wrote of the great American writer who asked him to be his literary executor, Edgar Allan Poe.

⟳ Montségur et Picaussel

Gettysburg is a small American town, a village really, surrounded by one of the great battlefields of human history. I moved here in 1986 and bought a house at the north edge of town, close to the campus of Gettysburg College, my place of employment. The battlefield proper is in the southern part of town, but in reality there is no line of demarcation. The battle took place everywhere here, and here at all because of a mundane oddity.

The southern troops, under the command of General Lee, were marching north on the west side of the first range of the Allegheny Mountains, specifically in the Shenandoah Valley and then in the Cumberland Valley. Their goal was to cross the bridges over the Susquehanna River in Harrisburg and then attack Washington from the north. By the time the army reached Pennsylvania, the troops were badly in need of shoes, and since Gettysburg was then known as a shoe-manufacturing town, Lee paused in Chambersburg to send a contingent of men east to procure the footwear.

The Union troops, meanwhile, were also marching north, but on the eastern side of the mountains, trying to stay approximately between the Confederate troops and the nation's capitol. When the Confederate shoe patrol arrived in Gettysburg, they ran into an advance battalion of Union soldiers, and the battle began. Thus it was that the Southern army entered Gettysburg from the northwest, and the Northern army entered from the southeast.

While waiting for the bulk of their forces to arrive, the Union troops set up defensive lines designed to delay the advance of the then more powerful Confederate force. I was out walking my dog a day or two after moving into my new house on the north side of Gettysburg when I discovered a small field commemorating the right flank of the Union line. The position, occupied by General Coster's New York regiment, the 134th, was overrun by General Early's Confederates, who were coming down from Harrisburg. Painted on a wall nearby was a mural illustrating the skirmish, and mounted before it was a plaque commemorating Coster's regiment: "This tablet marks the position where its casualties were greatest of any battle in which it was ever engaged. Loss at Gettysburg July 1st, 252." When I stood on that tiny field for the first time and read those words, I felt a strong kinship with those two hundred fifty-two boys, a connection through the soil. The same emotion came over me in 1994, in the Languedoc, near the tiny town of Lescale, when I happened upon a granite stone marking the graves of Jean Carbou and Joseph Lebret, young French partisans killed by the Nazis on the sixth of August, 1944.

I WAS ON SABBATICAL IN THE FALL OF 1994, AND MY WIFE Jean Straub and I had rented a house in southwestern

France. We had heard about this house during a visit with our friends Paul and Sue Zimmer, at their farm near the town of Soldiers Grove, Wisconsin: Soldiers Grove, where country boys from miles around gathered before heading off to the Civil War. They fought in the Shenandoah Valley, at the Wilderness, at Manassas, at Richmond, at Gettysburg.

In addition to having been a big-time mover and shaker in the publishing world, Paul Zimmer is the only important contemporary American poet to have been a catcher in a semipro baseball league, where he was known as "The Enforcer" and universally feared. As an infantryman in the US Army in the 1950s, he was one of the soldiers put in trenches close to a nuclear test explosion in the Nevada desert. When he talks, I listen, and this is what he said when I told him about my upcoming sabbatical: "You should spend some time in the South of France. My friend Susan Ludvigson—you must know Susan—owns a house there. She rented it to us once, and I am sure she would rent it to you." While I did not at that time actually *know* Susan, I knew *of* her—and of her husband, the fiction writer and essayist Scott Ely—and indeed, she was willing to rent the house to us sometime during the fall. We settled on all of October and some of November.

The house is located in Hameau de Campsadourny—*hameau* means hamlet—near the village of Puivert, in the foothills of the Pyrenees, not too far north of Spain and not too far west of the Mediterranean. Campsadourny appears on almost no maps, and Puivert did not appear on any of the large-scale maps I found in atlases at the college

library or in the travel section at Encore Books in Camp
Hill. Finally I bought, at a travel store in Bethesda, a small-
scale Michelin map for the Luchon-Andorre-Perpignan
region, and on it I found Puivert, located on national road
117, about halfway between Lavalanet and Quillan. We
are talking boondocks here, the road less traveled by, the
unbeaten track, the middle of nowhere; it was as though
an infinite number of roads diverged in a wood, and Jean
and I took the one Susan and Paul went down, and that
made enough difference that I am writing about it today.

WE SHOULD HAVE FLOWN TO TOULOUSE, BUT I HAD BUSI-
ness in Paris *et ses environs*, and so, eventually, we headed
south from San Benoît-sur-Loire (near the grave of Max
Jacob, a French poet also killed by the Nazis during the
Second World War), beginning our two-day drive to
Puivert—our *long* two-day drive to Puivert. At eight
o'clock on the evening of the second day, we were only
just approaching the city of Limoux—source of the first
"champagne," called Limoux Blanc—on the banks of the
River Aude, and there a bunch of roads diverged. The
highway continued south to Quillan; a road or two went
off to the east, into a region called the Corbières; another
went to the southwest—and that was our road, the short-
cut through Chalabre and on to Puivert.

By the time we were two miles out of Limoux, we felt
we had blundered upon *La rue destiné á la* nowhere *dans
la* dark-black-unending-empty-starless-uninhabited-and-
godforsaken *nuit*. Darkness is merely a concept outside
of the Languedoc, where every window in every house is

tightly shuttered, streetlights are rare in towns and non-existent in the country, and no one else goes anywhere at night. We drove into the tiny village of Puivert, population four hundred, at about ten; by eleven we had located the remnants of the ancient Lac de Puivert and the unmarked road diverging to Campsadourny; by eleven-thirty we had found the hamlet itself, dark and silent as death, all its twenty or thirty residents long gone to slumberland; by midnight we were laying our own weary heads on the musty pillows we found in Susan's house, which had not been opened for at least six months.

By six we were fully awake to the cries of number-less roosters and the putt-putting of a farmer's tractor just outside our back window. Stumbling up the stairs—the bedroom was on the second floor—we found the third-floor living room and kitchen; we found coffee; we found water and cups; we found a stove and a match; we found the door to a southern balcony; we stepped outside and uttered an involuntary but fervent *Sacré Bleu!* The houses across the road were two stories tall; ours was the highest point of view in town and we were astonished to see, beyond the tiled roofs, not only a valley full of farmlands and scattered hamlets, but the foothills of the Pyrenees, bathed in the morning sun, clothed in pine trees, haloed by wispy morning clouds—an unreal view, something akin to Paradise. When we leaned out and looked to our left, we saw on its own hill the ruined Château de Puivert, Puivert Castle, towering over everything. Without know-ing it, we were looking at two battlefields, places where terrible acts of cruelty had taken place.

A FADED NEWSPAPER CLIPPING THAT WE FOUND THAT first day in a cookbook told us that the château is where Susan married Scott, having discovered him and captured his heart some years after she had discovered the space that she turned into this house. Perhaps she chose the château for her wedding because it was, during the twelfth century, the site of the troubadour Court of Love, where the medieval poets gathered and held their competitions. Susan and Scott, poet and fiction writer, said their vows beneath the trefoil windows of the Musicians' Chamber, where the troubadours had earlier gathered to sing their poems.

That was about the only room left, as we soon discovered. Not only had the château been a residence, a writers' colony, and a court of love in its day, it had also been a fortress, a castle, a refuge upon a hill—unfortunately, a small hill. That is why, almost uniquely among medieval castles, the Château de Puivert was surrounded for protection by six outposts, six armed camps, now hamlets, each one named after its commanding officer: Hameau de Campsadourny, Hameau Camp-Saure, Hameau Camp Marcel, Hameau Campgast, Hameau Camp Sylvestre, Hameau Camp-Ferrier. We lived in one and could see three others from our balcony.

Mostly life was quiet in Puivert, indeed in all of the Languedoc, at least until early in the thirteenth century, when the château was captured by Simon de Montfort during the Albigensian Crusade. The Languedoc region comprises that part of southern France west of the Rhône River, where the language of the Provençal culture, the *langue d'oc,* was spoken. Known for the gentleness of its society, the Languedoc is where Catharism took greatest hold in France, if not in the entire world. More than seven hundred years before the Nazis occupied this land and killed Jean Carbou and Joseph Lebret at Lescale, the Pope's crusaders invaded the Languedoc and massacred thousands of devout Christian heretics, the Cathars.

WITH NO FORMAL ORGANIZATIONAL STRUCTURE OF ITS own—no churches, no services, no priests—Catharism was more a way of life than a religion. Its beliefs were spread not through proselytism but through the exemplary lives of its most devoted believers, ironically called *Perfects.* The name was bestowed upon the Cathars by the Roman Church; it does not mean that the Perfects were perfect, though they very much tried to be, but that each one of them was an *Hereticus Perfectus,* an absolute heretic. These heretics lived ascetic lives in the real world, avoiding not just sex but also touching; they told the truth at all times, no matter the cost; they were nonviolent and went willingly to their deaths rather than defend themselves or recant their faith; they kept no possessions and would not accept tithes; they believed in the sanctity of work, and gave their earnings to the poor. The Cathars were also remarkably tolerant and egalitarian; they believed in full equality between the genders (many Perfects were women); they did not condemn the relatively sinful behavior of simple believers; they did not condemn the beliefs of any other religion, including Roman Catholicism.

Although the Cathars condemned the Church's institutional venality and the immoral behavior of so many of its priests and other leaders, they were not in rebellion against the Church and had no desire to destroy it. Unfortunately, Pope Innocent III believed that the popularity and growth of Catharism was likely to weaken, however slightly, the power and prosperity of the Church. And so he took action. First he sent the Spanish friar Dominic to the Languedoc to try gentle persuasion. When this effort failed, the future Saint Dominic recommended a firmer approach: "I have begged and I have wept. But, as the saying goes in Spain, where a blessing has no effect, you need to wield the stick." This made perfect sense to Innocent. Thus it was that, in June 1209, approximately one hundred thousand crusaders gathered in Lyon, under the command of an unusually cruel man, Arnaud-Amaury, a papal legate and the Abbot of Cîteaux.

I LEARNED MOST OF THIS DURING OUR FIRST FEW DAYS in Campsadourny, by visiting the château and by reading some of the books in Susan and Scott's library. But even scholars and their scholarly consorts have to eat, and Jean had been doing some reading also, mostly in Susan's guidebooks. Forget three stars, two stars, one star; just to find a restaurant of any kind around there we needed to drive at least half an hour. And since we had to go somewhere, Jean reasoned, why not head south, toward the Pyrenees, which we wanted to see anyway? So at about seven o'clock one evening we again drove off into the smothering Languedocian dark, headed for the Hotel Bayle at Belcaire.

Our crossing of the valley was sedate, the valley that

had once been the floor of the Lac de Puivert, but when we started uphill, the road began to toss and turn, heave and squirm, causing our headlights to sweep from side to side, shining briefly on rocks and dirt and trees—and then on a single commemorative stone. We stopped, and I stood for the first time on the spot where Lebret and Carbou had died, "*mort pour la France,*" two months to the day after the Allied invasion at Normandy. This was news indeed; until that moment I had had no inkling that the Second World War had reached this far.

Back in the car we continued our climb through the trees; we passed a side road with a sign pointing toward the town of Lescale, and then, as we rounded a sharp curve, the mountainside fell away to our left, suddenly and precipitously, and a huge rock cliff appeared across the road directly in front of us. Happily, there also appeared a tunnel. We emerged from it into a thick forest growing out of rocks and rugged hills, Le Forêt de Picaussel, and from that we emerged, after another four or five kilometers, onto a high mountain plain, the Plateau de Sault. This dramatic landscape, we learned later, was where the local resistance group, Le Maquis de Picaussel, had established its enclave—to train, to hide, to store its supplies—and been attacked by the Germans.

Not that this was easy to find out; when I first asked our neighbors, no one had anything to say. Eventually a woman named Nicole, a volunteer at the local museum, told me to knock on her door at about eight o'clock that evening. When I did, she surreptitiously handed me a book—*Le Maquis de Picaussel* by Lucien Maury, "alias Frank"—and disappeared quickly back inside. Perhaps the war was not entirely over in Puivert; perhaps another of our neighbors had been not a freedom fighter but a collaborator.

So the Languedoc had been invaded not once but twice. The more I learned about these two events, the more similarities I found. To begin with, the citizens in both cases had been surprised in their homes, while going about their ordinary business. Frank had retired from the French Foreign Legion in 1940 and moved to Puivert to teach in the school at Lescale. On the morning of March 16, 1943, a simple schoolmaster, he was seized and questioned by the Gestapo: several parachutes bearing arms and supplies had mistakenly been dropped by the Allies on the area the night before; the real target had been a Maquis miles away. Frank was questioned closely, but could honestly say he knew nothing; by the end of the day, however, after his release, he had driven east to Quillan and made contact with the resistance organization there. They appointed him leader of a new unit to be established in the forest above Lescale.

The forces of Pope Innocent III began their crusade much more vigorously. After a long march from Lyon, the crusaders surrounded Béziers and demanded that all of the city's Cathars be turned over to them. When the citizens refused, Arnaud-Amaury ordered the extermination of everyone—Cathars and Catholics, men, women, and children: "Kill them all! God will recognize His own!" he shouted. In a letter to Innocent, he bragged: "Our forces put to the sword almost twenty thousand people."

Simon de Montfort was equally cruel and equally efficient. Shortly after he was made field commander, the crusaders captured the town of Bram and surrounded Cabaret, demanding its immediate surrender. Again the request was refused. So Simon had one hundred citizens of Bram released onto the streets of Cabaret—after ordering their eyes to be put out and their noses to be cut off. The people of Cabaret quickly surrendered. In June of 1210, Simon had his men burn one hundred forty Cathars at the stake in Minerve. The next spring, the crusaders captured the town of Lavour, raped and stoned Giralda de Laurac, the town's châtelaine, hanged her eighty knights, and burned another four hundred Cathars.

THE MAQUIS IN GENERAL WERE HARDER TO FIND THAN the Cathars. When active, they would gather in the shrubby mountain thickets from which they get their name; otherwise, they blended into the citizenry. Often the Germans, after some act of sabotage against them, would round up the citizens of a nearby town and conduct random executions until the perpetrators were turned over. On more than one occasion, everyone in a town was murdered. Because the occupation of the South began relatively late in the war, the Languedocians were less subject to this sort of thing than other Frenchmen. Still, they had their moments. For example, on April 13, 1944, shortly after the Allies had parachuted supplies (intentionally, this time) to the Maquis de Picaussel, a father and his son, both farmers, were seized at Hameau Camp Marcel, one of the towns visible from our balcony. The father tried to run and was shot to death. The son was executed at a concentration camp.

The Forêt de Picaussel was a nearly perfect location from which to operate a guerilla unit: to the west a series of rugged mountains provided an impassable barrier; to the north and east, the mountains fell away in dramatic cliffs. Only from the south, where the forest gives way to the Plateau de la Sault, was the Maquis at all vulnerable. Even there, however, the thick trees and rocky terrain provided considerable protection. The site had other advantages: eight hundred meters to the southeast of Lescale was a cave where the men could hide their weapons and seek shelter from the elements; springs provided plentiful water; all the volunteers were local men with an intimate knowledge of the landscape. From there on July 27, 1944, a band set out for the Gorges de Cascabel—on the River Aude, north of Alet-les-bains and Couiza—where they ambushed a German convoy, killing one of the enemy and injuring thirteen. On the third of August, another band journeyed to Limoux to steal a German shipment of tobacco for distribution to the French citizens.

Both of these raids took place after the Allies had invaded Normandy on June 6, 1944; General de Gaulle had ordered all resistance units throughout France to harass the Germans from the rear. German retaliation was swift; by the fifth of August, an enemy column on its way to attack the Maquis de Picaussel had already passed Lavalanet and was approaching Belesta. The next morning two resistance fighters were killed at Col de la Babourade, where Route 117 crosses a ridge, only a short jog from Hameau de Campsadourny. At four-thirty that afternoon, a German unit ambushed four Maquis on the road just below Lescale, killing Lebret and Carbou. Frank sent some men to retaliate, again at Col de la Babourade, and they wounded eighteen Germans.

By nightfall, the Germans had completely surrounded the forest. A radio message came over the BBC, signaling an Allied parachute drop: "The truth shines five times in all eyes." At about midnight, five British Halifaxes flew over the forest from the south, then turned straight back after locating the château (their landmark); one was shot down over Puivert, but the others dropped a thick cloud of arms, ammunition, and supplies to the Maquis, in preparation for the coming battle.

AT DAWN THE GERMANS SENT TWO MOTORIZED COLUMNS up the mountain, one on Route 120 from Babourade and one on the smaller road that leaves Puivert, passes by Hameau de Campsadourny, passes through both Hameau Camp Marcel and Lescale, then joins 120 just before the tunnel. When the columns reached that point, the Maquis set off the charges they had placed in the tunnel, forcing the Germans to retreat. The enemy reformed on the slopes below Lescale, began an artillery bombardment, and then attacked with infantry. Frank ordered the Maquis to hold their fire until the last moment, then signaled the fusillade that killed sixty Germans and drove the rest back down the mountain.

What had most surprised Frank was the direction of the German attack; rather than approach from the open plain to the south, they had tried to scale the rugged cliffs to the north. He concluded that the real assault would come at dawn the next day, from the south, where he knew German panzers were gathering. Guerrilla units do not stand and fight if they can avoid it; so after dark on the seventh of August, Frank ordered that all supplies be loaded on trucks in preparation for retreat toward the southwest. Not long after this convoy had passed the intersection at Espezel, the Germans sealed it off—but no matter. The remaining men were formed into two groups of one hundred fifty and marched silently out; heavy rain helped them pass unnoticed by Espezel, through Rodome, and on to Aunat, where they were picked up by other Maquis units and transported farther south to Quérigut. The injured were taken to the office of a friendly doctor in the town of Belcaire, where Jean and I had found our favorite restaurant.

The next morning the Germans threw everything they had at the southern edge of the Forêt de Picaussel; they drove quickly through the pine trees that the Maquis had felled across the road; they overran and burned several farmhouses along the way; they discovered the cave and captured the ruined tunnel; they reunited with the units still waiting below Lescale. But they killed no Frenchmen and took no prisoners, because no one was there. In frustration, they destroyed the town of Lescale.

To protect themselves from the crusaders, the Cathars also gathered on the mountaintops, in castles like the Château de Puivert, rock palaces perched on the highest crags. During our time in the Languedoc, we visited those at Puylaurens, Roquefixade, Peyrepertuse, Queribus, and—the most impressive and most famous of all—Montségur, which the Church at Rome variously called The Vatican of Heresy, The Dragon's Head, and Satan's Synagogue. Montségur was the only Cathar castle actually built by the Cathars; all the rest were the fortified homes of wealthy landowners who happened also to be Cathar believers. Montségur is located just south of Belesta, only ten kilometers west of Susan's house at Hameau de Campsadourny. Our favorite way of getting there was on the road that leaves Route 117 at Belesta and follows a small river into the rugged granite gorge lying at the bottom of the sheer cliffs that form the eastern side of the mountain.

When the crusade formally ended on April 12, 1229, pockets of Cathars remained sequestered in some of the castles. In November of that year, the Council of Toulouse established the Catholic Inquisition and put it into the hands of the Dominicans. Using tactics later to be adopted by the Gestapo, the Inquisitors hunted down many of these fugitives, questioned them, and—when they refused to repudiate their beliefs and return to the Mother Church—put them to death, often by burning at the stake. One by one the castles fell, until only Montségur and Queribus were left.

No doubt Montségur would have lasted longer had not its commander, Pierre-Roger de Mirapoix, led a group of medieval guerrillas on a raid to Avignonet, where they murdered several of the Inquisitors. The Archbishop of Narbonne called six thousand men to arms, and in the spring of 1243 they surrounded the castle. The Cathars held out for almost a year, thanks to their nearly impregnable position, but then the Inquisitors brought in a band of mountaineering mercenaries from Gascony, who improbably scaled the eastern face of the mountain. Approximately two hundred Cathars were captured. None of them would recant their faith. All of them were burned to death.

Among the Cathar guerrillas attacking Avignonet was Siscard de Puivert, son of the Lord of Puivert; his sister Saissa, a Perfect, was one of those burned at Montségur; both their parents, the Lord of Puivert and his wife Alpaïs, had received the *Consolamentum*—formal induction into Catharism—at Montségur, she in 1208 and he in 1232.

BY THE MIDDLE OF AUGUST 1944, WHEN THE MAQUIS de Picaussel returned to the Aude region from Quérigut, the Germans had seen the necessity of retreating from the Languedoc. In order to retrieve the huge amount of food and other supplies stored in their depot in Couiza, they dispatched a convoy of trucks and armored vehicles from Carcassonne. Couiza is located on the River Aude, just south of the Gorges de Cascabel, where the Maquis had earlier attacked a German convoy. Frank and his men returned to the scene of that battle and set up another ambush.

Guy David, their machine gunner, had a perfect view of the road from his position on the cliff to the east of the river; a group of men hid beside the road after planting several mines. The convoy had been halted and the Maquis were moving in when the Germans positioned a group of captive French civilians in front of themselves. Frank called for reinforcements; Charles Bournet and three other men maneuvered toward the rear of the convoy and began a suicidal skirmish designed to delay the Germans long enough for the new men to block the road at their rear by dynamiting a bridge farther up the river.

The tactic probably would have worked to perfection if the arriving unit, a group of twelve American parachutists under the command of Major Paul Swank, had had enough time to do its job. But Bournet and his men were overrun, and the Germans were able to mount a surprise attack on the second group of ambushers. Seeing the certain failure of his mission, Swank grabbed a Thompson submachine gun and fought the Germans alone, long enough for his men to escape. Eventually he was killed, and the Germans began their return to Carcassonne. Although the Maquis had failed in its attempt to destroy the convoy, their mission as a whole was a success. Rather than allowing the Germans to retrieve the supplies, they captured those supplies—one hundred eighty truckloads—for themselves.

Buried beneath a monument on the bank of the Aude, just one hundred meters downstream from where he had died, Paul Swank remains a hero to the Languedocians. Born on February 12, 1921, he graduated from Davidson College in June 1942 and joined the US Army on August 18. Trained as a clandestine fighter, he successfully completed sixteen missions behind German lines before dying during his seventeenth. In his book, Frank praises Paul Swank and many other Americans who gave their lives for France, while so many Frenchmen were—as Frank puts it—lounging by the fireside in their slippers.

JEAN AND I SPENT SIX WEEKS IN PUIVERT, SIX EXTRAORDI-
narily happy weeks in a marriage that was destined to fail.
On weekend mornings, as we sipped coffee on Susan's
balcony, gliders—pulled into the sky from a small airport
visible down the valley—would soar silently overhead,
gaining altitude on the air moving upward on the warm
southern slopes of the foothills. When the harvest moon
of October was at and near its full, the farmers would be
out all night bringing in the crops. One day a stray cat ap-
peared and lived with us for a week or two; I named him
Salvapoli, the Italian word for fox, in honor of his reddish
fur. I was fond of that cat and would have brought him
home to Gettysburg, but when the time came for us to
leave, I could not find him anywhere.

Searching for the Perfect Life: Secrets of the Amish

"Oh, I'm fine. But when I was trying to teach this morning, the pipes started knocking, and sometimes someone leaves a window open! Oh, my life is awful."

—CAROL RIFELJ, 1973

Today is December 17, 1998, and I am in the Sonoran desert, in Mexico, on the shore of the Sea of Cortez. To the east of me are mountains over which the sun is now rising; to the west are mountains beyond which the sun will set; in between are cacti, brush, palm trees, the water, flowers, and birds—especially birds—upon all of which the sun will shine brightly, all day long, as it does every day, all day long. I am in Paradise.

Except for the fire. When I awoke yesterday morning, the air in the condo was acrid and foul. I could not figure out why, but going out to do errands, I noticed smoke rising from behind a hill to the north. Because my Spanish is almost nonexistent, I could not ask anyone about the fire, so I drove up that way to take a look. I did not get very close, but judging by the terrain, I guessed it was a brush fire.

Last night I kept my windows closed, and now the wind

has moved around to the west and the air has cleared. Just a moment ago a small bird rested briefly on the railing of the balcony. Its wings and head were gray, and its breast was yellow. I know almost nothing about birds, but I can look things up, and I am pretty sure this was a MacGillivray's Warbler. Later today a pair of Magnificent Frigatebirds will hover overhead, their eyes scanning the surface of the water for a sign of something to eat. For all my life I have sought the perfect life, the perfect place. Perhaps I have found it here.

Except for the loneliness. But I came here for the solitude, to get a good start on a book I should have written years ago. I came here to get away from complications, from interruptions—from the office, the telephone, the fax machine; from e-mail, television, traffic, malls, Christmas shopping; from people, people, people. Writing is a solitary occupation, in many ways a monastic occupation, and I am lucky in never wanting much company. I am lucky, too, in loving my work, in taking as much pleasure from it as from playing tennis or seeing a good movie. When work is going well, life feels almost seamless, with all the parts working in harmony. It is nice to have that happening in a place as beautiful as this.

I HAD ALREADY BEGUN THINKING ABOUT THE PERFECT life before I came down here. What got me started was a book I bought last summer. When friends or relatives visit me in Gettysburg, I take them over to Lancaster County to look at the Amish. We drive straight through the town of Lancaster to Bird-In-Hand and on to Intercourse. We go in the shops and buy stuff, then drive around on the little roads and look at the farms and the gardens and the people, the horses and buggies. It makes a nice day. We end up at one of the local restaurants, where we eat chicken pot pie or roast beef, peas or beans or corn, mashed potatoes with lots of gravy, and a piece of apple pie for dessert. You can have it plain or with cheese or ice cream; the Amish don't care.

As tour guide, I used to enjoy making up amusing lies about the Amish while pretending that I knew what I was talking about. This was one of my most hilarious gigs. For example, once I claimed that the Amish are celibate, just like the Shakers. When someone in the car pointed out all the children running around, I insisted that the Amish take in delinquents from the cities, that they make big bucks that way.

At least I amused myself—some of the time. Increasingly, however, I began to feel guilty saying such things about a people who—I could tell even then—are sacrificing a lot in order to live a serious life, a life that to them may well be the perfect life. So I bought a book—*The Riddle of Amish Culture* by Donald B. Kraybill—and one day during the fall semester, after I had read about half of it, I decided as a lark to ask my students—some of them native Pennsylvanians, and one who wore a hair net very like those worn by Amish and Mennonite women—what they knew about the Amish.

"They ride around in buggies and have lousy taste in clothes."

"People say they speak Dutch, but really it's German."

"Most of them live in Ohio."

"They think that if you drive cars or use phones or tractors or electricity, you will go to hell."

"They look like Hasidic Jews."

"Instead of going to college, they take a year off to decide whether to go on being Amish."

"No, they take three years and just go crazy. They do drugs and sell coke."

"For recreation they raise barns."

"They don't get operations, they just die."

"They follow Christ's injunction not to bathe."

"They all have the same last name, Suckerman."

Almost forty-five years ago, when I was a thirteen-year-old kid in Minneapolis, I went into the closet of my room and wrote in pencil on the wall: "April 12, 1954—a perfect day." I remember enough youthful days like that to make me wonder now if I was living the perfect life back then, though for reasons that are a mystery to me I have come to think of Minneapolis almost with horror, and I have not been back there in years.

I taught at Michigan Technological University from 1964 to 1966, and those were good years, even though I had to work much too hard—or were those years good because I had to work so hard? But hard at teaching, with no time left for reading, much less writing anything that someone else would want to read. I needed a PhD to gain those advantages—and besides, the weather was really terrible in the Upper Peninsula—so off I went to North Carolina, where the weather was much better, and I earned the degree. But I had no money and lived the life of a galley slave as a teaching assistant for the English Department, a grader for the business school, and, in my last year, as editor of the *Carolina Quarterly*.

Vermont, though, that is where I truly found the perfect life—the landscape was beautiful, and I had a job I loved—until I was denied tenure and my bones began to freeze during the terrible winters. Houston was much better—I was quickly awarded tenure, found a new love, and was warm all the time. Too warm. Hot in fact. So now I live in Gettysburg and have the perfect job; I still teach, yes, but I get to edit and do lots of reading and writing. The winters are relatively mild, I love the students, and all my colleagues, all my friends in town, are first rate.

But the interruptions! Whenever I tried to start that book, I had a set of papers to grade, or decisions to make about manuscripts, or phone calls to answer! When I tried to drive through town, the streets were jammed with tourists! When I tried to think, the dog would bark, or someone would come into my office with a stack of letters to be signed! So I came down here to Paradise—though I am alone, and I really do not like the smoke from that fire.

ACTUALLY, I PICKED UP TWO BOOKS, THE SERIOUS ONE I am talking about and another one: I wanted to find some Amish jokes. There aren't any, but I did find a book of Pennsylvania Dutch jokes, and since the Amish speak Pennsylvania Dutch (a polyglot German dialect, as my student said), these jokes may be applied to them as well. Here are some things the Pennsylvania Dutch say in the course of their everyday lives:

"Lizzie, go in the house and smear Jackie all over with jam, a piece of bread."

"There's two roads to Hinkletown. They're both the same for far—but the south road is more the hill up."

"Amos, come from the woodpile in, Mom's on the table and Pop's et himself done already."

"Look the winder out and see what the weather gifs."

"I would have written or called sooner, but we don't liff where we did any more. We moved where we are at now."

"Look onct—is it rainin' out—it listens like. It wonders me if it don't gif a storm till evening."

"Is that you Hannah? Chust walk the fly-door in, the hook ain't at."

"Throw the cows over the fence some hay."

"You know Pop when I first vent to school I couldn't say norse or souse. Now I can say bose of em."

"My little Levi was out spritzin' the grass, and he stung his foot with a bee."

"Kissin' wears out, cookin' don't."

THE NAME SUCKERMAN IS MENTIONED NOWHERE IN Kraybill's book, but I did learn that 70 percent of the Amish have one or another of these six surnames: Stoltzfus (the most common), King, Fisher, Beiler, Esh, and Lapp. One mailman in Lancaster County was said to have three mailboxes on his route bearing the name Amos E. Stoltzfus and three bearing the name Elam S. Stoltzfus. The book taught me that and just about everything else I now know about the Amish.

For example, when the Amish arrived in Pennsylvania —they came from Alsace, though most of them were Swiss and German—they settled in what must have seemed like Paradise: the Amish are farmers, and Lancaster County is said to have the richest soil of any county in America. Although—given the persecution they had endured in Europe—anyplace in America would probably have seemed like Paradise to them.

Historically, the Amish are a splinter group of a splinter group of a splinter group from the original Christian tree, Catholicism. Eight years after the Reformation coalesced around the original splinterer, Martin Luther, a group of students in Zurich rebelled against their conservative Protestant leader, Ulrich Zwingli. In their eyes, Zwingli was still too fond of celebrating the Mass, was too closely in league with the civil authorities, and—most importantly—still advocated infant baptism, as did the Catholic Church. The neo-reformers—known as Anabaptists ("adult baptizers")—felt no one should be committed to church membership until they were old enough to make an informed choice. Because one of their early leaders was a man named Menno Simons, Anabaptists are sometimes called Mennonites, Menno-nites.

The Anabaptists immediately fell under persecution; one was killed for sedition only five months after the splintering. In the words of Kraybill, "Thousands of Anabaptists were executed by civil and religious authorities over the next two centuries. Anabaptist hunters were commissioned to torture, brand, burn, drown, imprison, dismember, and harass the religious heretics." Groups of believers naturally migrated to other countries—Alsace, Germany, the Netherlands, the Palatinate.

In the 1690s the Anabaptists who had gone to Alsace came under the leadership of Jacob Ammann, a strong-willed pastor with more splintering on his mind. Ammann disagreed with the Swiss ministers and their bishop, Hans Reist, over several issues, among them the degree to which fallen members should be disciplined. The standard punishment was a form of excommunication, banishment from all activities of the church. Ammann advocated taking the additional step of shunning, in which the members of the church were forbidden to have even casual social contact with the banned person. The additional pressure would return the fallen branch more quickly to the tree.

Ammann was a bold fellow: when his ideas were opposed by the Swiss leaders, he excommunicated all of them, and—though Ammann's followers apologized years later for his rash act—the new splinter has never returned to the older splinter of a splinter from the original tree. In honor of their leader, the newest rebels were called the Amish, Am(mann)-ish.

Ammann disagreed with other Mennonite practices and beliefs—for example, the Mennonite acceptance of a fashionable new invention: buttons. The Amish began to refer to the Mennonites as Button People, while they themselves were called Hook-and-Eyers. Ammann also believed that church members should ritualistically wash one another's feet, an act the Mennonites found regressive. Finally, though the men of both groups continued to shave their upper lips (moustaches were worn by the persecutors and thus represented the hated military and its government), the Mennonites had taken to trimming their beards, an act the Amish felt was contrary to the intent of God; if He had wanted the faithful to trim their beards, He would Himself have restricted their growth.

I LOVE AMMANN'S INSANE GESTURE, EXCOMMUNICATING his superiors and colleagues as though he were expelling them from his church rather than himself from theirs. What a madman. I equally relish the disagreements over feet and buttons and beards—especially when coupled with the fact that Amish men do get haircuts but Amish women may not. I mean, if God is so concerned with the free growth of facial hair—though not all of it!—then shouldn't He be concerned with head hair as well? And the Amish haircut: the wife literally puts a bowl over her husband's head and cuts off all the hair that hangs below.

I have found some other Amish distinctions that do not make a lot of sense to me, distinctions that seem based more upon appearances than on anything more substantial: for example, the Amish farm with horses, while *moderns* (the rest of us) use tractors; the Amish generate their own electricity using windmills, while moderns purchase energy from public utilities; the Amish all dress the same, while moderns dress fashionably. All of these distinctions seem relatively trivial to me.

And I have to admit that I find some of the conveniences scorned by the Amish helpful in my own attempts to live an uncomplicated life: moderns use microwaves, the Amish don't; moderns use vacuum cleaners, the Amish don't; moderns use blenders, food processors, toasters, doorbells, air conditioners, and light bulbs, the Amish don't. Similarly, the Amish don't hire babysitters or eat in restaurants, but I do. The Amish don't go to health spas, car washes, barber shops, basketball arenas, or football stadiums, and I happily go, occasionally, to all of these.

So what makes me admire the Amish way of life? Not the specific prohibitions of all these services, places, and devices, but the compelling reason that lies behind them: by avoiding most of what constitutes modern life, the Amish are better able to preserve their own way of life. Amish families spend more time together than modern families do; they live in quieter houses and go to bed earlier. Such things as poverty, crime, violence, murder, and divorce are virtually unknown in Amish communities. Their old are not condemned to hospitals and retirement homes; their young are not warehoused in consolidated schools, factories, and prisons. They have almost no mental illness; suicide is nearly unknown among them. They are free from consumer debt, from the frustrations of traffic, from anxiety over what to wear, from endless strings of commercials on TV, from boring jobs, from bureaucratic regulations.

Where the Amish have obedience, moderns have disobedience; where the Amish have humility, moderns have pride; where the Amish go slow and value work, moderns go fast and value leisure time; where the Amish practice thrift, moderns practice luxury; where the Amish stay at home, moderns go to Disneyland; where the Amish practice sacrifice, self-denial, and discipline, moderns pursue pleasure, extravagance, and ease. The Amish look to their churches and discover community, a sense of identity; moderns look to their individual selves and achieve alienation.

When a psychologist administered a standardized personality profile test to a group of Amish, he found them to be "quiet, friendly, responsible, and conscientious." They work "devotedly...to meet [their] obligations and serve [their] friends and school" and are "patient with detail and routine." They are "loyal, considerate, concerned with how other people feel even when they are in the wrong."

THERE ARE, HOWEVER, TWO THINGS I DO NOT MUCH LIKE about the Amish way of life. One of them—the subservient role of the Amish woman—seems to lie behind the last of the Pennsylvania Dutch jokes I quoted earlier: "Kissin' wears out, cookin' don't." Amish women are forbidden from being ministers, deacons, or bishops, but they are responsible for all the cooking, all the housework, and most of the child-raising. They also are expected to maintain flower and vegetable gardens and to help out in the fields when they have some free time. I wonder when that is.

My other reservation concerns the Amish way of education. Donald B. Kraybill explains it well, while also seeing the Amish rationale: "By encouraging a practical education that ends with eighth grade, the Amish are, in essence, restricting consciousness. Critical, rational analysis that fosters independent thought would surely spur individualism and fragment the community. Limiting the flow of ideas and banning threatening worldviews through ethnic schooling is essential to preserve the Amish way of life."

Before 1972, Amish children were educated in public schools and were legally required to attend through high school. In that year their petition to be released from these requirements was ruled on by the Supreme Court, with Chief Justice Warren Burger delivering the opinion: "[T]here can be no assumption that today's majority is 'right' and the Amish and others are 'wrong.' A way of life that is odd or even erratic but interferes with no rights or interests of others is not to be condemned because it is different."

I love Justice Burger's ringing affirmation of the American freedom to be different, to follow an uncommon path. He is describing what is, for me, perhaps the most important component of a perfect life. And yet this very freedom, extended to the larger Amish group, is what restricts the freedom of every individual Amish child to be different, to follow an uncommon path. I feel this personally: had I been educated under the Amish system, I cannot imagine that I would be speculating today on the perfection of my own way of life, for without the power of "critical, rational analysis," without "independent thought," without "[un]restricted consciousness" my life today would not be worth living.

Despite this intense sheltering, Amish young people are—surprisingly, I think—allowed to experience modern life before having to decide about baptism. Though not all of them do the three years of hard drugs envisioned by my student, they are said to go to parties and drink alcohol, to engage in rowdiness, to travel to the city to see movies. And yet fully 80 percent of these "rowdy youth[s] . . . settle down to become humble Amish adults." Kraybill goes on to say that the Amish feel "a minimal dosage of worldliness . . . strengthens resistance in adulthood." My own feeling is this: If Amish young people are unthinking puppets in the hands of their parents and their community, then modern young people are puppets in the hands of Joe Camel and Bud Light.

WHEN I WAS BACK IN GETTYSBURG AND FEELING TRAPPED by my hectic schedule, I envied the Amish for living what looked like the perfect life. Now I am in Mexico and living what surely is the perfect life for me. Except. Except for that fire, except for the loneliness, except that I miss my wife, except that I will miss being with my family and friends at Christmas. And I miss my dog.

None of this surprises me, for none of it is new. Like you, I have always tried to live the perfect life, and sometimes I have thought I had attained it. But I had not. And if I tried to live the Amish life, which seems so perfect for them, I would not be happy; that life would be even less perfect for me than the life I live in Gettysburg—or the lives I once lived in Minnesota, Michigan, North Carolina, and Vermont. And if I have found perfection where I am now, among the birds and the mountains, on the beach and under the sun, doing the work that I love, I know that I have achieved it by giving up a great many other, important things.

So what am I to conclude, after all this laborious rumination? Maybe this: that I have spent a lot of my time thinking about the perfect life from the wrong perspective. What is most obvious to me now is that I *am* living the perfect life, and have been all along. What else could I possibly call a life that allows me to sit around thinking about this subject? I also know that Louis Simpson was right when he said in one of his poems: "It's not a bad life. Nothing is." Whatever life I may be living now or at any time in the past or future is bound to be better than the alternative, which is no life at all.

⤚ Alejandro y los Condominios Pilar

I went to the place in Mexico, the place in Sonora, the place on the Sea of Cortez—to San Carlos and the *Condominios Pilar*—to work and to be alone; to be alone and to get started on a book; to rebuild my mental and physical health and to be alone; to be alone and away from the hassles, the telephones, the obligations, the deadlines of everyday life. I cooked my own food and washed my own dishes and swept my own floor and laundered my own clothes (in the kitchen sink) and got myself into bed early and out of bed early, and I worked hard all the time, unless I was busy doing something else, and then I did that hard as well, and I was entirely cool with all this because I was happy to be in Paradise and living the perfect life—and wasn't it about time, for the sake of Martha and Mary and Joseph and Little Baby Jesus, so help me God—and one of the other things I did was hang with Alejandro some, watched him conduct his business, and I used that as a way to learn more about this part of the world.

Alejandro spends his days driving around the village of San Carlos selling produce, mostly to gringos but also to restaurants and local citizens. Before meeting him two years before this trip, I had heard about him from Jean, my wife at the time, who thought him one of the most colorful characters in a colorful place, and from some of her relatives, who seemed to think his prices were too high. What I think is, yes, he is colorful, and, no, I don't care what he charges, because his prices are comparable to those at Ley's, the supermarket in Guaymas, and his produce is fresher, and I would much rather give my money to him than to the Safeway Corporation, which owns the Ley's chain and would never stand around in the sun shooting the breeze with me, as Alejandro often happily did.

AFTER A FEW DAYS IN PARADISE, I COULD NOT DECIDE whether I would rather be a dolphin or a *pelicano*. I fell in love with the pelicans right away, those goofy and scraggly and awkward and uncoordinated sojourners on land who miraculously become "among the most graceful of birds in the air: riding air currents over coastal wave lines; soaring high over the ocean; migrating effortlessly on extended wings"—until they spot some hoard of delectably edible fish creatures they want to eat, and then they will dive, suddenly and unpredictably, straight down into the ocean from ten or twenty feet up; the pouch beneath their beaks will hold three gallons of water, which they let dribble and gush out, leaving the fish behind to be eaten. One day the wind was blowing in, hard, from the south, from straight out at sea, and the pelicans retreated into the *estero* beside the condominiums and played there all day, in groups of twelve or fifteen. A group would rest for five seconds, maybe ten, then fly up en masse, go a short distance, and plunge, again en masse but from a height of only four or five feet, into the water as though they wanted to dive for delectably edible fish creatures but had forgotten how.

Watching this performance—they were obviously playing, just screwing around—I formed the notion that the only way pelicans knew how to land, so to speak, in the water was by plunging and splashing, but on another day, jogging my way on the beach back from the place I call Araby, I saw lots of pelicans skimming, one by one or in flocks or gaggles or coveys or mere twosomes, across the surface of the sea, then deftly and gracefully landing on the water, without a splash. And so, I decided that in my next life I would come back as a *pelicano*.

ALEJANDRO SHOWED UP AT ABOUT SIX O'CLOCK THE EVE-ning of my second day there; I was sitting on the patio reading a book and wondering idly what to have for dinner, when I heard his trademark call, "Hello?...Hello?...Hello?...," coming closer as he wound his way among the buildings, and then, as he came around the final corner and saw me, "*Hola, Señor,* you need any vegetables? Fruits? Best price in San Carlos. I got shrimp, very fresh," and then, coming still closer and recognizing me, "Ah, *buenas tardes, Señor,* welcome back. It is good to see you. What you need?"

I followed him to his ancient truck and spent *mucho dinero*, three hundred sixty pesos—thirty-six dollars, ten pesos to the dollar—buying avocados and limes and lettuce and grapefruits and onions and garlic, a long rope of it, and honey, a bottle of the finest—"All vitamins, no water, no sugar added, pure, I sell to restaurants downtown"—and cilantro and scallions—"here, smell, very flavorful"—and papayas and tomatoes and everything else he offered me, orange juice and tortillas and new potatoes, and then we stood a while shooting the breeze, and I asked him if I could follow him around a bit during the next few weeks, watch him do his work, maybe find some answers to the mysteries of Sonoran Mexico, maybe write a little something about it, and he said, "Sure, no problem. The first thing, *Señor*"—getting started right away—"if you sell food you gotta have everything clean. Here, look," and he opened the door on the passenger side of his truck and made me look at the floor, feel under the seat: the floor was worn, rusted, but I could find no dirt, no dust, no gum wrappers, no used tissues, no dog hair, nothing unwanted anywhere. He unloads the truck every morning, five-thirty, and washes everything, top to bottom. Neighbor kids help him for odd coins, and his wife, but his own children—four of them, boys seven and twelve, girls thirteen and sixteen—help only when he is in dire straits: "They don't want this business. They go to school, want something better. Everybody wants to progress," he said, and I certainly agreed with that.

IN ONE OF MY RECURRENT DREAMS, I AM WALKING ACROSS a college campus, hurrying to get to a place called, and who knows why, Nicholson Hall before the bookstore closes, taking longer and longer steps until I discover that I can fly, upright, my feet six or eight inches above the ground, steering by leaning this way or that, something like a helicopter turned on its tail. The sense of freedom, power, maneuverability, is wonderful, and sometimes I get confused during the course of a normal day and think that, if I just take long enough steps on my way downtown for coffee in the morning or over to the convenience store to pick up the newspaper, I will lift off and begin to fly, but it never happens, and now I am becoming cynical, and whenever this dream begins I warn my sleeping self, sure that I am not sleeping, not dreaming, "Listen, Pal, we have been through this before, and you know you can't really fly, so don't even think about lifting off and soaring all the way to the bookstore," but then I walk faster and take longer steps and behold, suddenly I am airborne, flying again, floating gracefully over the acorns and the cracks in the sidewalks, avoiding by leaning this way and that the people and the trees and the trash cans, and then I say to myself, joyfully, ecstatically, "No, I was wrong, it is true, I *can* fly!"—and I do, all night long, until that awful moment when I wake once more to the bleak Pennsylvania dawn and gradually realize that, "Damn, it was only a dream."

WHEN ALEJANDRO WAS STILL A BOY, HIS FATHER BROUGHT the family north to Guaymas and started selling seafood —shrimp, fish, clams. Alejandro helped the family out by selling the tamales made by his mother. When he was twenty-two years old, in 1971, Alejandro got a job in San Carlos, cleaning up at Shangri-La, one of the bars, and that is where he began learning English, by listening to the gringos while he swept the floor. Three months later he was promoted to bartender, and in 1978 he quit and started selling shrimp, like his father. He bought the truck and expanded into produce. His mother still makes the tamales that he sells; she makes the tortillas, too, and squeezes all the juice, orange and grapefruit.

Alejandro works seven days a week—full days in the winter, when lots of people are around, and half-days in the summer, when not so many people are around. Not many were around during the first part of my stay, the part before Christmas, but starting on about the twenty-third, the *Condominios* really started filling up. Alejandro had warned me of this, naturally in an effort to sell me something: "At Christmas, many people come here, lots of parties. I have best lobster. You buy now and save. Only two hundred pesos per bag. Here, look, beautiful . . . and shrimp! I have shrimp also, only one hundred thirty." I had come there to be alone, etc., so I wasn't planning any parties, but I did buy a bag of his lobster tails and got about ten meals out of it, two dollars per meal, not bad.

WE WERE STANDING BESIDE HIS TRUCK PARKED NEAR THE *banco* one afternoon when a woman walked up, not from the bank or the parking lot, but from across the street. If you are a gringo staying in San Carlos and you need produce and you happen to see Alejandro's truck, you must stop at that moment and buy: "I don't have a strict schedule," he says, "but I have my places to sell—the *banco*, the old marina, the Pilar, the dry storage, Rosa's, and out toward Club Med, the Marina Real, the trailer parks—but if one place is slow I go on, and if a place is busy I stay until it slows down, and I am never sure where I will go today." The woman bought lettuce, tomatoes, and radishes —twelve pesos in all—but refused the orange juice offered by Alejandro: "I still haven't squeezed all those oranges I bought from you last week," she said, so I asked if she thought her juice was better than Alejandro's mama's, and the woman said, "No, it's not as good. But squeezing it is the only exercise I get here in Paradise."

A gringo came out of the bank and opened the door of his car. "Hello," announced Alejandro, taking a few steps into the parking lot, "I got fruit, vegetables, shrimp. What you need?" The guy thought for a moment and said, "Orange juice." Alejandro returned to the truck and grabbed two half-gallons out of his cooler: "Here you go, best in San Carlos, fifty pesos, I only sell by the gallon." The guy paid and, pulling away, joked, "How much is your vodka?" He should have said, "No, I only need a half-gallon," because then Alejandro would have said, "Sure, OK," and sold him a half-gallon.

I asked Alejandro the secret to his success: "You have to convince them to buy. And you have to concentrate on business. When I am down here doing this, it is all I think about. It's what I do. I like what I do." Another time he told me his motto, his mantra, his philosophy of life: "You gotta have quality products. You gotta be honest—to the customers and to yourself. Have patience. Be ambitious. Work hard."

Be clever. One afternoon at the condos, I arrived at Alejandro's truck just as a man was paying for a whole bunch of stuff with a handful of bills, but Alejandro did not have exact change and owed the man six pesos, so he said, "Here, take two cantaloupes," but the man decided he would rather have a dozen tortillas, ten pesos a dozen, so Alejandro earned an extra four pesos by not having the correct change. "This business," he said, "sometimes you sell a lot, but mostly you just get by."

I was fixed on the *pelicanos*, but then on one of my morning walks, I joined a group of dolphins, some grown-up and some still little, who were grazing for delectably edible fish creatures and goofing around fifteen or twenty feet off shore, parallel to the beach, coming up out of the water to breathe, nosing back under to push and rub against each other, nuzzling and cuddling and racing ahead and circling back around, following a shoal of fish or maybe looking for one, or just happy with themselves during their morning constitutional, their beach parade—I also part of the parade, or pretending to be, pacing right along with them—and then I decided that, no, I would come back as a dolphin instead.

I looked them up in my battered and old portable *New Columbia Encyclopedia* and learned that I will, in my next life—or in the one after that, if I do come back as a pelican next time—be happier in the company of dolphins than I am now in the company of most humans, for dolphins are smarter ("In relation to body size, the brain of the adult [dolphin]... is twice as convoluted [as that of man] and possesses 1½ times as many cells"); are able "to converse and... convey instructions"; are "capable of imitation and memorization [and]... demonstrate foresight, learn from observation, communicate experience, solve complex problems, perform elaborate tasks, and learn multiple procedures simultaneously." Best of all, from my Paradise-and-perfect-life-seeking perspective, "Their so-called training is in fact a discipline structured around play, using their natural behavior as the basis for involved maneuvers, [which] they ... perform primarily for their own enjoyment," quite unlike nearly all the humans I know, for whom work is a solemn and puritanical duty worth doing only for the money it brings.

ALEJANDRO TOLD ME HE HAS A SMALL BANK ACCOUNT— "You have to have a little money in case you need a tire or something"—and wishes he could save enough for a new truck, but he doesn't have the customers, too few gringos are coming down: "Things are very bad in San Carlos. There are no people. You know, everything has to move, and now it costs more money. I make a living but a lot of Mexicans are very poor. It is very hard on them." The Mexican economy has been terrible for years, and usually that works to the advantage of gringos, who ought to be traveling to take advantage of the exchange rate, so I figured there had to be another reason for the bad times in San Carlos, and I asked Alejandro if there was ever a time when a lot of people had been around, spending a lot of money, and he answered, "1976 was the best year—'74, '75, and '76 were all good, but especially '76."

The dates made sense to me. A few days earlier, rummaging through a pile of old magazines in the condo, I had come across a mysterious document—printed out by dot-matrix printer on the old-style computer paper, with perforations and holes along the sides—that tried to explain "the problems of" the *Condominios Pilar*, oddities I had thought of as among the typical features of this part of the world: for example, the totally incongruous, mile-long dirt road that branches off toward the condos from the wanting-to-be-glorious-but-failing highway that runs from Guaymas to San Carlos, the *Avenida Manlio Fabio Beltrances*, not to mention all the other unpaved roads that also branch off—from the *Avenida*, from the road to the Pilar, from one another—and head out into the vast empty desert spaces that lie between the *Condominios* and the place I call Araby, three miles away, which marks the outermost edge of the town of San Carlos—and wandering around this huge area one day I came across ruined brick *casitas*, lines of fallen concrete utility poles, large semi-excavated areas that looked like the start to foundations, not to mention spiders, scorpions, snakes, creosote bushes, cacti, and an area where what is obviously the sewage of the *Condominios Pilar* flows onto the desert sands. The bushes are bigger there, and are shaded by trees.

As for the place I call Araby, I call it Araby because each of its condo units looks, from the *Avenida*, like a miniature Muslim mosque with an air-conditioning unit perched awkwardly on top, though the sign out front says the proper name is *Champs*—says so ironically, I think, for though there are twenty or thirty of these units, I have never seen more than three or four vehicles parked in there—and one afternoon during my six-mile run I decided to take an archeological break by going in and having a look around. From the side facing the water, Araby presents a decorated wall surmounted by colonnades and a sun-bathing area. I entered through a broken gate onto a walkway that ran through a short tunnel beneath the sun-bathing deck before opening onto a huge, unfinished, and obviously-never-used courtyard containing two swimming pools, one olympic size and one smaller; two or three bars from which I am sure no drinks were ever served; an area painted for shuffleboard beside the beginnings of what looked to be a small miniature golf course; a tennis court; bath houses and restrooms, and though all these pieces were more or less in place, construction had stopped before the finishing touches were applied; despite the three or four cars out by the road, this courtyard was deserted and falling to rubble.

OFTEN MY FLYING DREAM ENDS BADLY: HAVING REACHED the bookstore in Nicholson Hall, I walk up and down the aisles searching, but with no idea of what I want, and as I search, more and more people appear in the aisles, spontaneously appear, blocking my way, retarding my progress, preventing me from doing whatever I hurried there to do, and I never know what that is and never find out, because from then on in this dream I wander, on foot, from one confusing and crowded scene to another, never arriving anywhere, never knowing where I want to arrive, and whenever I wake up from this recurrent nightmare, I wander irresolutely all day, wondering what I am always wanting and why I want it, wondering what I am always needing to get done and why I need to do it, wondering why I seem unable quite to start whatever it is I want to finish doing.

ALL OF THE EMPTINESS FROM THE MOUTH OF THE *ESTERO* TO the edge of Araby, including the *Condominios Pilar,* is what remains of something called Villa del Mar, "a first-class subdivision" dreamed up in the early 1970s by a Tucson developer named Bill Pickens and designed to include "hotels, apartments, condos, and single-family housing." The success or failure of this grand plan hinged on laws governing the Mexican Land Reform, which required that at least 51 percent of all commercial developments be owned by Mexican citizens. In this case the land was owned by a Mexican named Juan Manuel Salsedo, and that was meant to satisfy—in the official documents at least—the law, and probably it would have except that nothing official in Mexico gets done without the *mordida,* the paying of bribes to dozens, perhaps even hundreds, of bureaucrats, and many years into this process but before its end, Salsedo died, leaving everything he owned to his son, and his son pulled out of the project, for reasons un-known, sending the American investors back to Tucson, broke, in the year of our lord, 1976.

Meanwhile, back in 1974 Bill Pickens had wanted a showplace to entice prospective buyers and investors, so he arranged for a Mexican developer to build the *Condo-minios Pilar,* and this was before any of the infrastructure was in place—the entrance road, the sewage system, the water system, the electric and telephone lines, every-thing—and it was still not in place by the time the condos were finished and the project was dead in the water, and that is why those problems exist today.

THE FINAL THING I WANTED TO DO DURING MY STAY IN San Carlos was meet Alejandro in the parking lot by appointment at Ley's early one morning so I could follow him to the municipal market in Guaymas and watch him shop for his daily inventory, but though I waited at Ley's for almost an hour, he never appeared, and though I went on alone to the market and wandered in the crowded, smoky darkness for an hour, I did not find him there either, and though I looked for him later that day, and all the next day, and the next, I never did find him and never did finish off my project by meeting his family, taking some pictures, and finally understanding what I wanted from, what was really going on in, my little patch of Paradise, my mysterious, ragged, irresolute, and unfinished area of Sonoran Mexico.

A Boy, a Girl, Then and Now

I am certain that I remember this. I don't see why I would have made it up or dreamed it. Four years old, too young to be so far from home without a parent near, you are playing by the creek where it runs parallel to Morgan Avenue, near Fifty-Second Street, with another kid. It must be late spring. The day is warm, and the creek is high.

The other kid's house is on Morgan Avenue, just across the street from the creek. Now his father is there, in his pajamas, home from work sick with the flu or something, running along the creek, reaching toward it, out of breath.

His boy is in the water, floating downstream, drowned. The father runs, dressed only in pajamas, out of breath, feverish and sweating, frantic, reaching, trying to save his boy, but the boy has drowned.

You are standing there. You see the father. I see him too, but that is all that I can see. If the kid did drown, and I am certain that he did, then there must have been police, an ambulance, lots of people, something in the paper. But I cannot remember any of that. What I remember is that

135

father in his pajamas running along the creek, unable to reach his son, who has fallen in the creek and drowned.

THIS IS CLEARER. SOME YEARS LATER YOU ARE IN THE car with Stevie and his father, driving around Lake Harriet, down by the pavilion and the dock for the sailboats. A crowd of people is gathered near the dock. Something has happened to draw them there. Stevie's father parks, and the three of you get out of the car to look.

A teenage boy has been electrocuted while working on the bottom of a sailboat with an electric sander. He is lying on the grass, near the boat. You are on the sidewalk, outside the chain-link fence. When someone standing near the body shifts position, you catch a glimpse of the boy's face, which is flushed a deep, purplish blue.

ANOTHER TIME STEVIE'S FATHER PULLS INTO THE GROUNDS of Lakewood Cemetery and parks. I think the point of this trip is to pick up Stevie's mother somewhere else, and you are early, so there is time to kill. As the three of you sit in the lower parking lot of that cemetery, Stevie's father points to a building, says it is the crematorium, explains what they do in there.

YEARS EARLIER, PERHAPS AROUND THE TIME OF KINDER- garten or first grade, you are in a Sunday school class. You ask the teacher, a woman, what happens when a person dies, and she says, "To find that out, you and I would have to go into a dark room together." She is talking about death. She is saying she could teach you about death if the two of you were in a dark room alone.

All of these events are part of my experience. They are as true as I can tell them.

You are in fourth grade, sitting at your desk, just in front of the one occupied by a kid named Jim. You begin to cry. When the teacher asks why, you say, "My stomach hurts." When she asks why again, you say, "Jim hit me." It isn't true. You have appendicitis.

The teacher carries you down to the nurse's office. The nurse calls your mother, and your mother takes you to the hospital. Another nurse says, "This is ether," and puts a bitter-smelling rag over your mouth and nose. You breathe, and the rag becomes an endless blanket, black and red, patterned like a checkerboard. You push at the blanket, pull it away from your face, but it keeps revolving up and away, turns into the space before you, an endless field, and you see yourself, a speck floating out there, far away.

Then you are lying in a bed. Your mother is sitting in a chair, her hand on your forehead. You ask her why the bed is wet, and she pulls aside the covers. You are lying in blood.

Instead of putting a rag on your mouth and nose, this time they stick a needle in your stomach. You ask the nurse when they are going to take the needle out, and she says they took it out a long time ago. All the nurses are women.

The kids in your fourth-grade class write letters saying they hope you feel better. You return to school on a winter day. You are skinny now. Jim knocks you down and sits on your stomach. The girls dance around, waving their pencils.

YOU ARE FALLING ASLEEP ALONEIN YOUR MOTHER'S BED, I don't know why. You have a bed of your own. Suddenly light, massive amounts of reddish-orange light, comes into the room through the drawn shades. I think you are nine years old. Maybe eight.

Your oldest sister's boyfriend is there. He goes in his car to see what happened. An airplane, a trainer in the Army Air Corps, on its way back to Wold Chamberlain Field, had clipped the water tower with a wing. The pilot had tried to make it to the creek, where nobody lived, but the plane fell short, hit a house, burned three houses, killed a lot of people in three families.

You go there with some other kids. You walk through the house on the corner, you see the kitchen table with the cokes still sitting on it. Even the bottles are burned.

WHAT EXACTLY WERE YOU DOING THERE? I KNOW YOU were walking the dog, Allen's dog Sheba, but why there, between those houses, past those windows with the shades half pulled?

Does an alley run up there? I don't remember, but

probably it does. All the alleys in that neighborhood run north and south, the length of the blocks. Never the width. So let's say there is an alley, and when you get to the end of the house, the fancy one that faces the creek, you turn left down the alley.

Then you must have crossed the street and turned left again, for you are walking on the grass beside the street, parallel to the creek. It is like a park there. Somebody must have mowed the grass along the sides of the creek, for miles and miles.

A car is parked there in the dark, but before you reach it, a man comes running across the street and hits you in the face with the butt-end of a shotgun.

Then another man is standing by that car, on the driver's side with the door open, and a woman is screaming, wailing really, "Let's go, right now. We've got to get out of here. I'm scared." I think you begged them not to go—I know you reached out to her for help—but they left.

Another woman appears, pulls the man away. Then you are in a bathroom, and she is washing the blood from your face. Allen looks in at you from the hallway. The woman says she is sorry this happened.

The man says he did the right thing, but maybe to the wrong person. He thought you were bigger. He did not know what you were doing behind his house, near his windows. Margie, your next-door neighbor, finds out that the man owns a bar down on Washington Avenue, the Stockholm, maybe a hangout for the mob. She says he is probably afraid all the time, of things we would know nothing about.

You are taken to the hospital, the emergency room.

You stay home from school, hiding your cuts and your black eyes. The girl named Janine something, whose friend Meredith you think is cute, walks past your house one afternoon on her way home from school. A sisterly girl. You are sitting on the stoop. She is shocked to see your face.

Your dad tells this story over cards, and one of his friends, the car-painting king, says, "Go see my lawyer." You go, the three of you, your mother and your father and you, but the lawyer says there isn't a case, that the man had a right to protect his property, that you should not have been walking by his windows. It was your fault.

But you were not on the man's property when he hit you with the shotgun. You were walking along the creek with your friend and his dog. Maybe he was a mob lawyer. I don't know. Given what I learned later about the car-painting king, that would not be much of a stretch.

So what were you doing back there, by those windows? It is really not a good place to be walking a dog. You must have known that. Maybe you and Allen made that part up after the fact. Maybe you were glancing in those windows, hoping to see a woman undressing.

He hit you in the face with a shotgun. You were fourteen, just a kid. He wanted to kill you.

TWELVE? YOU RIDE YOUR BIKE DOWN THE ALLEY BEHIND your house, fast as always. You turn through the gate by the driveway, go down the steep little hill, aim for the other gate, end up on the ground with a rope around your neck. The bike rolls on alone.

The rope is for the dog, tied to a metal ring and hanging down from an aluminum clothes line. There is no good reason why your neck and it are in exactly the same place at the same time, both in just the right position for the rope to wrap around your neck and pull you off your bike.

But they are and it does, and now your neck has a bad rope burn running all the way around it. Your mother applies salve and pins a cloth loosely around your neck.

TWELVE? THIRTEEN? YOU RIDE YOUR BIKE TO SOME KID'S house. You are with a friend, his last name might be Rosen, but you don't know him very well. He is from your neighborhood, and he knows the kid with the house. That is why you are there.

You are in the backyard, the three of you, talking while swinging a tire hanging from a rope, like playing catch with a ball.

You look away, and the tire hits the back of your left hand, not hard but it hurts like crazy. You get on your bike and head toward home. At the top of the long hill on Fifty-third Street, you stop, not knowing how to get down with just one hand for the brakes.

A car pulls up. It is a guy named Tom, older, Errol's age, one of his friends. He asks what's wrong, puts your bike in his trunk, takes you home.

Then you are sitting on the floor of the hallway, across from the door to the bathroom. Your father comes by, angry, interrupted. You ask him to take you to the doctor. He says he's not taking you anywhere at that time of night. You mutter the word *bastard*. He smacks you with the back of his right hand, bounces your head off the wall. In the morning he takes you to the emergency room. The doctor puts on a cast.

A couple of weeks later, you are watching a baseball game with Tommy, Margie's son. An older kid comes by, asks "Did she roll over on you?" You don't know what he is talking about.

Seventh grade, Ramsey Junior High. Vern Mikkle-sen, the power forward for the Minneapolis Lakers, is your gym teacher, though this is not relevant to the story. Your mother drives you and your sister to school.

After you and your sister get out of the car on Fifti-eth Street, your mother pulls away from the curb without looking. At that precise moment, Mrs. Goldhirsh, driving a yellow '53 Buick, is passing by, bringing her son Jerry to school. She cannot help but bump your mother's car, a black '52 Chevrolet.

"That god-damn Mrs. Goldhirsh," your mother says, after you get home from school. It was Mrs. Goldhirsh's fault.

Another day you arrive home, and there is no mother. She has had a heart attack and was taken to the hospital in an ambulance. She is going to die. Frieda, the woman from next door—the other side, Errol's mother—gives you the news and takes you to her house.

Frieda's sister is there. She sits you down on a chair in Frieda's living room and explains that it is your fault. You haven't been nice to your mother. All the trouble you have caused her over the years has put a terrible strain on her heart, and now she is going to die.

It is a theory; that woman knows nothing about you and your family, but you do not know that then. It is your fault. Your mother is going to die.

When your mother comes home from the hospital, nothing is the same. She cannot cook, cannot clean, cannot climb stairs, cannot change the beds, cannot do the laundry. Your father has a job. Your oldest sister is married and gone. You and your older sister get to do these things. That's the way it is from now on.

Now I know it wasn't a heart attack. Chronic pancreatitis, but no one figured that out for years. It hurts like hell, pancreatitis. I had it myself a couple of years ago, a single attack. The treatment is not to eat. They put you in the hospital and feed you through a tube for five days. Then they give you some Jell-O.

But your mother keeps eating, she keeps being sick. She is sick from that moment forward until her death, almost forty years later.

She was not a happy woman. You were not a happy boy.

WHEN IT COMES TO THE PAST, NOBODY IS RIGHT, AND nobody is wrong. What you have experienced is what you have experienced. What you think is true is true, and what you think is false is false. There is no truth outside of anybody that is true for everybody. Time exists in packets, and the packets seem to arrive in a certain order, but they don't have to. You can die before you are born, if you prefer it that way. You can bring your packets back up and arrange them in whatever order you choose. Then you can rearrange them. You can become a different person. The packets are the only things that are real or true. But sometimes there is evidence.

Albuquerque, New Mexico, 1990–1995

You don't know why your younger sister stays home, but she does. It is always she, never you, never your youngest sister. The two of you are the ones that your mother takes with her when she goes.

She takes you to a bar, usually the same bar but sometimes a different one. She leaves you on the sidewalk outside, you and your youngest sister. You have just turned five, and your youngest sister is about two and a half. You sit on the sidewalk, maybe you walk around some, maybe you play clapping games, maybe you just watch the cars go by. People also walk by, and some of them enter the bar. Every hour or two your mother comes out with two cokes, one for you and one for your youngest sister.

The hours pass. It is not cold out there. Albuquerque in August is warm, even at night, even on the sidewalk in front of the bar. Especially on the sidewalk in front of the bar.

Then she comes out with some other people, no cokes but a couple of six-packs of beer. They cross the street and go into the park. You take your sister's hand and tag along. They drink and argue, yelling loud, then louder.

Someone pulls your mother's hair, punches her in the face, and she falls to the ground. They start to kick. You are still holding your youngest sister's hand. You walk out of the park and down the street. You enter an alley. You won't let go of her hand.

A car pulls up, then another, then a third. There are lots of lights, red and blue and white. The people who get out of the cars are policemen. One of them is a woman, not your mother. They put you and your sister in one of the cars and take you to a place where there are things to eat, lights and beds. You keep holding onto your youngest sister's hand. You ask them where your younger sister is. They tell you she is all right. She will be there in the morning. They give you food. You eat and sleep.

In the morning the door opens. Your younger sister sees you and runs in. You see her and run to her. The three of you hug. You won't let go. Two weeks later you meet your new mother, and you go home with her. You don't go back. You are never going back.

YOU WERE EIGHT MONTHS OLD WHEN SOMEBODY FIRST called and made "a referral alleging physical neglect," alleging "nutritional deprivation, unhealthy environment, parenting problems, and lack of supervision," alleging that "the mother was drinking and fell and the child was hit on the head," that "the mother remained asleep but the child was crying," that you were "not cared for and may have asthma," that your diapers had not been changed.

That was in April. By the next April, when the next call arrived, you had a sister to take care of, a half-sister, and your mother had been "arrested for domestic violence and was intoxicated. She may have hit [you] during the dispute. She was charged with child endangerment. There were no bruises or marks on either child but were both [sic] dirty and smelled strongly of cigarette smoke."

A year after that, again in April, when you and your first sister had another half-sister to take care of, "the Department received a referral alleging physical abuse. There was a fight between [your] mother and [her] boyfriend. The boyfriend picked up [your youngest sister] and threatened to snap her neck." The Department talked to your mother. She said she "was no longer living with" her boyfriend. She said she was "providing for [your] basic needs." So "the case was unsubstantiated," and no action was taken.

The next April passed without trouble, but then in July another call came in, "a referral alleging physical neglect." After leaving "the two youngest children with a friend," your mother "took [you] with her to a movie, ran away from the boyfriend, and [you were] found outside her friend's house the next morning." During her interview, your mother explained why she had taken you along on her date. She said you were "attached to [her]"; you were her "best friend." Did she take you along when she ran from the boyfriend? When did she drop you off on that doorstep? Where did she go then? By the time the Department arrived, all three of you, your sisters and you, "were running high fevers and were taken to [the hospital] by paramedics. The case was substantiated for physical neglect and medical neglect. The case was closed."

The following March another call was received, alleging that your "mother leaves [you] children for weeks at a time with her father," alleging that you did "not have adequate clothing," but "the mother was unable to be found with the children and the case was closed." Your mother's father, actually her stepfather, is your grandfather, actually your stepgrandfather.

In June of the same year, "the Department received a referral alleging": that the three of you were suffering "physical abuse, emotional abuse, physical and emotional neglect." But though you and your sisters "were seen outside with little or no clothing, were dirty, and hair not combed," the "neighbors did not indicate concern," and your "grandfather denied [the] allegations." A week later "the Department took a 48-hour Hold. The children were seen by a doctor and were placed in foster care [for two days, then] returned home." Your "mother did not follow through" with treatment, and "the case was closed with substantiated neglect."

Then in early September "the Department received a referral on the children alleging physical and emotional abuse." Five days later, "the Department received [another] referral on the children alleging emotional abuse and physical and emotional neglect." It said, "The mother was extremely intoxicated and she had been in a fight with three alleged drug dealers. The children were present during the fight. The children indicated they were living in the streets." This is how your mother explained, in her interview, what happened: "I got into a fight. Actually, I was jumped. The fact that I was fighting they said was child neglect. I had been at the park earlier. I guess I had been drinking. Before I knew it, a lady and her black friend took off with one of my kids. I called the cops and they took me to the hospital. The cops took my children.

They want me to do urinalysis and some other things. I don't have an alcohol problem because I quit. I quit about a week ago. I don't have a drug problem."

All the charges were substantiated. The case was not closed.

Salt Lake City, Utah, 2000

As the car pulls up, you see three sets of eyes so brown they are black staring at you from the back seat. You are going to the baseball game, you are meeting the children. The middle one had written you a letter. She wanted this to happen.

I remember this clearly, but I am not sure of the exact date. I hope it was in May rather than in April, because of the abuse the girls had suffered, because of the many referrals in April.

The girls are nine, eight, and seven. The older two are matter-of-fact, almost blasé. The youngest one holds back, clings to her adoptive mother. As you cross the street, the oldest takes your hand.

In the seventh inning, the youngest one crawls up onto your lap. She stays there for the rest of the game. She has been there, in a manner of speaking, ever since.

Gettysburg, Pennsylvania, 2000–2001

It is raining, a lousy day. Everyone is cooped up in the new house, "the pond house," and you have made plans for indoor tennis. Lucky you.

The girls' adoptive mother suggests a drive to Washington. Maybe it would be better to get everyone out of the house. You cancel tennis, I do not remember how reluctantly.

The little ones get into the car, but the oldest girl refuses. Her mother pleads and reasons and cajoles. You plead and reason and cajole. The girl spits and hisses and runs to hide. You find her in a closet. She runs again. It is a big house. You are frustrated, becoming angry. Her mother is angry.

You find her in the attic, but at the bottom of the back staircase. She is curled up beside a sealed door. Her eyes flash in the dark. She won't come out.

You go down. The staircase is narrow, hasn't been used in years. You grab her by the wrist, try to get her to stand up. She resists. You put your hands beneath her arms, pull her up the stairs.

She fights with you. Her nails are long, like claws, and she digs them into your forearms. She screams, she wails, she is going to call the authorities. You pick her up. She cannot be in charge.

She continues to fight and scratch, a feral cat. You grab her hands as you carry her, you squeeze them hard. Then you squeeze them harder. You want to throw her to the floor. You concentrate on breathing.

You get her in the car. By the time you reach Frederick, she is herself. When you cross the streets in Washington, she instinctively takes your hand. This has always been the most striking thing, the oldest girl taking your hand.

⬱ Where Does Love Go?

I left home on the second of January in the year 2000, and on that first day of travel, I heard the gist of a millennium-eve story on the radio. Many years ago a group of high school boys agreed that they would meet on the steps of (I think it was) the state capitol at midnight on the thirty-first of December, 1999. To commemorate their sincerity, each of them had the number 9 tattooed somewhere on his body; I don't know where, probably different places, depending on personal preference. I was born on the ninth of October and have always considered nine to be my lucky number; had I been a member of that group, I would have had my nine tattooed on the top of my left wrist, facing me, right where I have never wanted to wear a wristwatch.

One member of that original group—I did not catch his name, but I think he lives now in either New Jersey or New York—drove half-way across America to honor what he felt was a sacred obligation to his mates. But no one else showed up. The story on the radio was about him; it was a short piece, and he was not quoted. I do not know how old he is, nor how lonely he felt standing on those steps. As for where this took place, I know only that it was somewhere in America.

I vaguely recall making a similar arrangement in high school, though with only one of my friends. I suppose we were wondering about the afterlife, and we agreed that, at a certain time on the Wednesday of the second week after the first one of us had died, we would meet. I don't remember with whom I made this agreement, nor where we were to meet, but I am sure we specified a place: were I arranging this kind of assignation today, I think I would specify India. I have always wanted to visit India, and the prospects for reincarnation seem especially good over there—not that we were talking about reincarnation, though we may have been, for all I remember. I should have written it all down. And then I would have had to have saved it all these years.

THOUGH THE TRIP I WAS STARTING WAS TO BE NEARLY identical to the one I took at almost this same time last year—I was off to Mexico to enjoy another of my writing retreats—two things were different: this time I was driving rather than flying, and this time I set out in an odd rush, given how long—over a year—I had been planning to go. The change to driving was a practical decision; I have more free time this year, and I wanted to have my own car. But the hurry to go, the compulsion I felt to get away immediately after making my final decision to go, is a more complicated matter and will not be easy to explain. But as I drove on that first day, one song among

the many I heard on my car's CD player—"America," by
Paul Simon—haunted my imagination, as it often has in
the past. The speaker and his friend are riding on a bus,
searching for something. This is how the song ends:

> "Kathy, I'm lost," I said,
> Though I knew she was sleeping.
> "I'm empty and aching and
> I don't know why."
> Counting the cars on the New Jersey Turnpike,
> They've all come to look for America.

He is empty and aching, lost, while Kathy sleeps on, oblivious to the depth of his feelings. Probably she does not mean anything by her inattention, but for some reason—her tiredness, perhaps her own sense of emptiness—she has left him alone.

So what is he, the speaker of that song, the guy setting out on his trip, searching for? I am struck by the loneliness of the last four lines of the stanza, the loneliness of the cars, the loneliness of the act of counting them, of the notion that all of those cars, that all of the people driving those cars, are out there looking for...well, for something Paul Simon calls America. Not for a dinette set, not for a good movie, not for a hidden paradise in Mexico, but for America. Perhaps each of them is seeking his or her own America, or is seeking the soul of America, the soul of his or her own America. Or perhaps each of them is seeking his or her own soul. But we—the singer and I—are not in any of those cars; he is riding on a bus looking out at them, and I am driving my own car, setting out on a trip across nearly the entire breadth of America. Perhaps what we are searching for is riding in one, or in all, of those other cars; perhaps it is a person, or several persons; perhaps a soul, or several souls.

On the second day of my trip, I worried about the weather. My car is sporty and fast; it has never been good on snow or ice. According to the weather reports I was hearing from various stations on the radio, a storm was sweeping east across America, a cold front dropping lots of moisture—rain at first, then ice and snow. The temperature when I left Gettysburg promised to rise into the sixties. By the time I stopped for gas somewhere in Ohio, I had to remove some clothes. The unusual warmth, which continued as I drove through Indiana, Illinois, Missouri, and into Kansas, made me even more nervous about what was coming.

Sometime during the middle of the second day, the weather did change: rain began to fall, and eventually the rain turned to snow. I put my sweatshirt back on, turned up the heat. The snow gradually thickened, and though most of it blew off of the highway at first, eventually some of it began to stick. I went by trucks spreading sand and salt, and some of them were even plowing.

But my progress was still good. I tried to stay in the tracks made by the semis, and I drove slowly and with serious concentration. I was halfway across Kansas when I stopped for dinner at an Applebee's Restaurant; I ate a rib-eye steak, medium rare, and a salad—I forget what kind of dressing—and drank a glass of water. By the time

I had finished eating, the precipitation had stopped, and the roads seemed almost entirely clear. It was dark, but only eight o'clock, and I decided to make another hundred miles before finding a place to sleep.

I made it only as far as the bridge over exit 127 on Interstate 70, maybe twenty or thirty miles from Applebee's. Because the road seemed so dry and clear, I had begun to feel comfortable driving and thought that maybe two hundred more miles was not out of reach. After a while I even started going faster and passed a truck or two; there were very few other vehicles on the road. But there was ice on that bridge. When I noticed this, I tried to do the right things—basically, make no changes at all and perhaps start a short prayer—but the car began to skid to the left. I must have overreacted, because a second later I was skidding violently toward the right and had lost all control.

However fast I was going was too fast, much too fast. The car was spinning in a clockwise direction, and suddenly the guardrail at the side of the bridge was rushing toward me. My first thought was for the car, my beautiful car. Then I realized that I was about to die—I was going that fast, headed straight for the guardrail and a drop of who knows how many feet to the highway below. I was about to meet my soul, about to find America.

The car stopped moving. I had a headache and was still alive, but the car was full of acrid smoke. Somehow a fire had started, and I had to get out in a hurry or be burned to death. The door opened when I pulled on the handle, and I stumbled onto the shoulder of the highway. The car was facing in the same direction I had been headed, west, as though I had simply pulled over to park. As a truck passed by, I gave a feeble wave, thinking the driver would stop, but he roared on past.

Shaking, dazed, still standing beside the open door, I noticed that the smoke was almost gone; there appeared to be no fire. Then I saw the deflated air bag, hanging from the center of the steering wheel. It must have deployed when I hit the guardrail, and what I had thought was smoke was the gas from the air bag. I sat back down. Some of the eight file boxes I was carrying in the back seat—full of books, papers, and supplies—had broken open, and stuff was strewn everywhere.

Eventually, I noticed a motel on the south side of the freeway, back across the bridge, in the direction I had come from. I was going to walk down there and ask for help, but then I thought I would try the car. It was still running and seemed to work just fine, so I backed slowly down an entrance ramp and made my way to that motel.

When I asked the woman at the desk if she had a room, she laughed and said, "We haven't got a thing, hon, and I doubt you'll find one anywhere in town with this weather." I said I just had an accident. "Oh, yeah" she said, "the last guy who came in said he saw someone having trouble up on the bridge." Then she looked at me. After a pause, she picked up the phone and found me a room at the Kansas Kountry Inn, just up the road.

The phone book said I was in WaKeeney. I found a listing for the B and C Body Shop and called the night number. A woman named Cindy answered and told me to come on over in the morning, and Terry, her husband, would do what he could to get me back on the road. The room was $36.70, plus $14.05 for a couple of long-distance phone calls, and the temporary repair on the lights and turn signals came to $65.

THE LAST TIME I WROTE ABOUT BEING HERE IN MEXICO, I mentioned how much I was missing my dog, Simon. This time I have several photos of him with me, but I still miss him, maybe more. And I still miss Pilar, my former dog, whom we had put to sleep a couple of years ago when he was in great pain from the cancer that was consuming him. I had my arm around him when the shot was administered, and he was looking into my eyes. Within seconds, he became still; his eyes were still locked on mine, and it took me a moment to realize that he was gone. His gaze is mine to interpret, and I think he was not blaming me for what was happening to him; instead I think he was looking at me with love, affirming our connection, trying to make it endure. But I cannot reach him; even if he is out there somewhere—in his America, or mine, or everyone's —he is lost to me forever.

When I was ten years old, I had a dog named Lady, I am pretty sure a boy dog. He went everywhere with me, and I loved him without reservation. One afternoon I was playing touch football with some other kids in the middle of a street, Logan Avenue South, two blocks from my home. A car came along, and we all moved to the sides. But Lady had to bark at that car—he barked at every car that ever went by—and though the car was barely moving, Lady fell beneath the wheels and was run over. I ran over to him. He stood up for a moment and grabbed my hand in his mouth—not to bite but to pray, to beseech, to beg me somehow to hold him back, to keep him from dying.

Even though my parents bought a new dog right away, I was inconsolable. And when I think about it now, I am inconsolable once more, even today, writing these words in my own private paradise. For no matter how hard I try, I cannot reach Lady; the car that killed him, the car that carries him now, is still going, and I have no idea where. Were I a different person entirely, I might consult a pet psychic to help me, for pet psychics are all the rage, according to *USA Today*, at least in some parts of America and with some types of Americans. A woman named Barbara Radin Fox, for example, wanted to do something extraordinary on her fiftieth birthday. On her fortieth she had hired a fortune teller, and ten years later the question naturally arose, "How can I top that?" She decided to hire a dog psychic so she could channel to Cuddles, her dead golden retriever: "Cuddles sent us messages about the meaning of his death and gave all of us advice on how to live our lives. All of it really made sense. It was really incredible. Otherwise, we are sane, rational people." I don't know who the other people she refers to are; probably the guests at her party.

According to Arthur Myers, author of the book *Communicating with Animals*, many animal lovers follow up on their first experience with dog psychic communication by taking workshops. Eventually, he says, "They practically all can talk to dead pets," which is worth doing because, as Steve Huneck (illustrator of a book called *My Dog's Brain*) says, "Dogs absolutely have a spirit." Besides that, "People and animals come together for a purpose," says Karen Wrigley of Manassas, Virginia. "There is some growth or teaching to be gained, a sense of closure or affirmation." A high point in Wrigley's career came when she chatted with a dead iguana, who said that "he loves running free." Another specialist in communicating with dead pets, Sananjaleen June Hughes, explains: "Your animal is a tiny, weeny piece of your guardian angel. If I tell people, 'My dog is an angel,' they raise an eyebrow. But if you ask people, 'Can an angel do anything it wants?' they say, 'Well of course it can.'"

MY FRIEND STANLEY W. LINDBERG DIED ON THE EIGHteenth of January in this year of 2000. I received the news here in Mexico in an e-mail on the twentieth. Though we had worked together some, by mail, when he was an editor at the *Ohio Review,* Stan and I first met at the Modern Language Association convention in New York in 1976, when I appeared at his hotel room to offer myself as a regular reviewer of poetry for the *Georgia Review,* of which Stan had just become editor. We had a nice talk, but he did not give an answer to my request until he had thought about it for six or eight months, and then he said yes. Over the next eleven years, I wrote forty-four essay-reviews on contemporary poetry for him, each on approximately five books, each approximately twenty-five manuscript pages long, meaning something like two hundred twenty books covered in about eleven hundred manuscript pages. Our arrangement came to an end in 1987, shortly after—with considerable help from Stan—I was chosen to be the founding editor of the *Gettysburg Review.*

Almost everything I know about editing and publishing a literary journal, I learned from Stan. At the time I took this job he invited me to visit him in Georgia, where he gave me what amounted to a short course in editing. And for years after that, I called him frequently, to seek (and accept) his advice on such matters as circulation, distribution, budget, submissions policies, relations with other units of the campus (including how to deal with administrators), anything and everything. Stan's grasp of the fine points of all matters practical was always better than mine, and he never led me astray. I do remember one time during the early days of the *Gettysburg Review* when I made him angry: in accepting a few poems by an important American poet that both Stan and I admired, I naively suggested that the writer send the others to the *Georgia Review*, where I was sure they would be accepted. When the poet acted on this suggestion, Stan called to ask, "Are you not satisfied with one magazine to edit? Do you want to take over the *Georgia Review* also?"

Stan was a chain-smoker for most of his life, and eventually he developed emphysema. He fought the disease with great courage for several years, still working, thinking, advising, remaining a friend to American writers. I was unable to make it back to Georgia for his funeral last weekend, and I cannot accept the fact that he is dead. Even now I want to reach for the phone to call him up, find out what he is thinking, ask him what I should do, ask him where he is going or has gone, what kind of car he is driving now.

SHORTLY AFTER HE WROTE "THE ASSIGNATION," ONE OF his best poems, James Wright sent a copy of it, along with several others, to his friend Donald Hall, then poetry editor of the *Paris Review*. Hall had a lot of suggestions for how the other poems could be revised, but "The Assignation" he pronounced nearly perfect. James Wright was obsessed with the subject of death, as most poets are. The poem is written from the perspective of a woman whose husband or lover made this promise as she was dying:

> You sat beside the bed, you took my hands;
> And when I lay beyond all speech, you said,
> You swore to love me after I was dead,
> To meet me in a grove and love me still,
> Love the white air, the shadow where it lay.

Now she has been dead for a year or more, and the appointed time has arrived. She rises from her grave and makes her way to the grove (I love the way the two words work together), but finds herself again alone:

> O then it was you I waited for, to hold
> The soft leaves of my bones between your hands
> And warm them back to life, to fashion wands
> Out of my shining arms. O it was you
> I loved before my dying and long after,
> You, you, I could not find. The air fell softer,
> My snatch of breath gave out, but no one blew
> My name in hallowed weeds.

The loneliness, the isolation, is heartbreaking. In many of his poems, James Wright longs to establish communication, contact, between the living and the dead, and always the effort ends in failure.

The situation in this poem is similar to the plan I laid out with my friend in high school: the persons involved were to meet at a prearranged place, at a prearranged time. In the poem both characters obviously know when the woman died, where they should meet. But what if the survivor never learns of the other's death, forgets his name, forgets the time and the place? Perhaps my friend died years ago, perhaps shortly after we made our pact. I imagine the loneliness he must have felt at missing this one last opportunity to participate in the realm of the living. I feel guilty for my inattention, and then I think: Our agreement was flawed! We should not have specified a place, probably not a time either! We should just have agreed that the dead person would find the living person; surely the dead inherently possess the necessary knowledge, or they have easy ways of finding it out. He should have come to find me. Then neither of us would have had to remain lonely, aching, empty, and lost, counting the cars on all the major highways in America.

But what am I thinking? If it were possible for the two of us, callow high school kids, to have established and carried out such a plan, then surely others, hundreds and thousands of others, would have already tried it, and some of those sojourners would have written about their success. Communication between the living and the dead would be an everyday topic, an everyday occurrence. We would not have to rely on pet psychics or on any other kind of psychics; we would be doing this regularly, without hindrance, without restraint. But we aren't.

ONE OF THE DIFFERENCES BETWEEN MUSIC AND POETRY is illustrated by the first two of the four Paul Simon lines that I quoted. When I speak the words "Kathy, I'm lost, I said, though I knew she was sleeping." I almost cannot make them sound like poetry. When Simon sings them—putting no pause on the first comma, a normal pause on the second, and an elongated pause on the third comma, while also using the melody—the effect is pure poetry. The words at the beginning of another song—Harry Nilsson's "One"—are more obviously poetic, though alone they have nothing like the emotional power they have when Aimee Mann sings them, a capella, at the beginning of the recent film *Magnolia*:

> One is the loneliest number that you'll ever do.
> Two can be as bad as one,
> It's the loneliest number since the number one.

Part of the difference is again in the timing, the exaggerated pause that Aimee Mann inserts in the second line between the first two words, her almost nonexistent pause at the end of that line. The rest comes about because of the music itself, the feeling inherent in the progression of pure sound. And I love the simplistic wording of the third line, which grows more meaningful each time I hear it.

In all of his writings, Edgar Allan Poe associates music —a music unsullied by words—with what he called the "supernal" realm, the realm of the supernatural, of the spiritual, of the eternal, the beautiful, the unchanging. Any lesser art is time bound and of the earth, though poetry, because of the way it expresses language musically, can at least approach the supernal, hint at its glories. Poe's beautiful young mother died before his eyes when he was just two years old. In "The Philosophy of Composition," Poe says that the most affecting subject possible to poetry is "the death of a beautiful young woman," particularly when expressed by the man who loved—still loves—her. When the protagonist of a Poe poem or tale searches for "supernal beauty," he is actually trying to regain his dead beloved, Poe's mother. The only way that can be achieved is through the agency of death. But either the story ends just before the death of the protagonist, in which case his apotheosis is perhaps imminent, though for the reader it remains merely a hoped-for impossibility—or the story ends with the death and apotheosis of someone else, but the enduring and unending sorrow of the bereaved protagonist. Such is the power of music to the poet Edgar Allan Poe.

LAST SUMMER A WOMAN I HAD BEEN IN LOVE WITH FOR thirty years died, at the age of eighty-six, of breast cancer. Given the difference in our ages, she was something like a mother to me, the sort of mother most of us can find, if at all, only outside of our own families. Although I knew of her illness when it was diagnosed, four years ago, news of her sudden steep decline did not come until she was already gone. Gone. Gone where? Not saying goodbye to her opened a hole that will never close, somewhere in my heart. I do not know whether she missed me during those last months, thought about me, longed to hold my hand, but I do know that, wherever she may now be driving her old Plymouth station wagon, she perfectly understands and forgives my absence, as she always understood and forgave.

Perhaps that hole in my heart is actually a tunnel—something like the one over the road in the forest of Picaussel, above the village of Puivert, in France, in the foothills of the Pyrenees, the tunnel beside which I found the graves of those two kids, members of the French underground, killed fighting the Germans during World War II—a tunnel through which passes a highway, the highway traversed by the dead. Maybe that is where they are driving now, or riding, on their way to somewhere or nowhere, all the lonely dead—the sleeping and the dead—for whom I ache in my exile and my emptiness. My mother drives there in her old Chevy, cursing the "sons of bitches" who caused all her accidents; my father drives there, chain-smoking his cigarettes, and my Aunt Mayme, and my Uncle Francis; Pilar rides there, sleeping peacefully, and Lady, coughing blood from his crushed lungs; and Bill, drowning in the bathtub with his heart attack; and Larry, alone on the floor with his death for four days; and Chris, the loneliest and most recent one of all. And Stan, chain-smoking his cigarettes and coughing his blood. And Marion, my beloved Marion, whose every word was a poem, whose every poem was a song.

Acknowledgments

The essays in this collection were originally published as "Editor's Pages" in the *Gettysburg Review;* all have been extensively revised. "In Love Begins Responsibility" was republished in part in *Harper's.* Several friends and colleagues have read and suggested changes either to individual essays or to the collection, and I would like to thank in particular Kathryn Rhett, Mark Drew, Mindy Wilson, Jeff Mock, Emily Ruark Clarke, and Jean Straub. During the time of composition, I was awarded two sabbaticals by Gettysburg College. I thank the committees that made these awards and the now-former provosts who supervised them, Baird Tipson and Daniel DeNicola. I thank Stanley Plumly, Rebecca McClanahan, Suzannah Lessard, and Kathryn Rhett for their kind words. I thank Lucy Gardner Carson for her careful copyediting, Jim Schley for his overseeing of the manuscript during production, and Jeffrey Levine for his role as publisher and editor-in-chief of Tupelo Press. Cassandra Cleghorn I thank for her late-night phone call telling me of the acceptance of the manuscript. Others who provided support, knowingly or not, include Jack Ryan, Fritz Gaenslen, Fred Leebron, Hope Maxwell Snyder, Floyd Collins, Dick Allen, Richard Frost, Lorin Rees, Michael Waters, Paul Zimmer, and of course all the others whom I have neglected to mention.

CPSIA information can be obtained at www.ICGtesting.com
Printed in the USA
BVOW01s1729211013

334067BV00001BA/1/P